CASUALTIES

OF

THE CALL

Author's Autograph

_____

_____

_____

_____

_____

_____

_____

_____

_____

_____

_____

_____

_____

_____

_____

_____

_____

_____

_____

_____

Elder Tommy Arbuckle

"Casualties of The Call"

Preface

So there I was, finally at the moment I had been waiting for—my interview to become an Elder at my local church. As I sat there, answering questions about my calling and discussing how the senior leaders could support me, everything felt like it was falling into place. But then came the final question from my senior pastor that would stay with me even to this day. *"Are you going to be okay?"* At first, I wasn't sure if I had heard him correctly, so I asked him to repeat it. He said, *"Are you going to be okay?"* His question left me puzzled as it didn't make sense to me. I didn't quite understand why he was asking, so I asked, *"What do you mean?"* He lowered his head, looked away, and said, *"There are just some things that come with this position that I hope you'll be okay with."* So I pressed him further, *"Like what?"* He lifted his head and looked me in the eyes with the most somber expression I had ever seen. After a brief pause, he said, *"It's really hard to even put into words, it's just some things."* I was speechless. When I was younger, there was an old saying my grandmother used to say whenever I asked her questions but couldn't quite grasp the answers she gave: She would say, *"You'll understand it better, by and by."*

I invite each of you reading this to walk with me as I try to help you understand what I didn't know then but have come to know now about what they really meant.

Table of Contents

"Casualties of The Call"

Foreword

Reflecting on the lives of Paul and Silas in **Acts 16:24-28**, it recounts a powerful moment where God's intention was not simply to deliver them from their physical imprisonment but to make Himself known in the midst of their trial. This divine intervention brought about a deliverance that impacted everyone present, revealing a glorious plan far greater than an escape. Like Paul and Silas, I, too, have encountered moments where God stepped into the **"room"** of my life, shaking the very foundation of my circumstances to reveal His purposes.

One such moment occurred when I was on a flight returning to the United States from a trip to Israel. While on a plane at 37,000 feet, God chose to have a closed session with me. There were no distractions, no interruptions—just His voice cutting through the noise of the aircraft and my thoughts. He spoke one word: **"Ransom."** This word catalyzed a profound and transformative encounter as God began to unfold His perspective on events in my life—both past and present.

Isaiah 43:3 declares, *"For I am the Lord your God, the Holy One of Israel, your Savior; I give Egypt for your ransom, Cush and Seba in exchange for you"* (**NIV**). This verse reveals the depth of God's love and the extraordinary lengths He goes to redeem

His chosen people. A ransom is a price paid to secure release, and in His sovereignty, God has allowed certain people, situations, and storms to be part of His divine plan to redeem and elevate those of us He has called. He uses sacrifices in exchange for what is necessary to fulfill His purposes in our lives.

As I reflected on the word *"ransom,"* God began to unveil the purpose behind the storms, chaos, pain, and wounds I thought could've been avoided. I wrestled with the reality of those I unintentionally hurt along the way—people who misunderstood my intentions and were wounded not by any malice but by my immaturity. I sometimes lacked the wisdom to explain, reason, or communicate what was happening in my pursuit of destiny. Yet, His response was clear: these moments were neither random nor purposeless. They were deliberate acts of divine orchestration. Lives were impacted, and painful experiences were allowed—not to break me but to shape me for the next level of my development. Though I grieved for those affected by my journey, God reminded me of His sovereignty, saying, *"I am the Lord, their shepherd; I will take care of them. These things were necessary for you to move to the next place, to benefit the lives I have predestined you to touch."* With this revelation, I saw my experiences differently—not as senseless casualties but as a part of a greater purpose only God could cause someone to understand.

The concept of ransom highlights the sacrifices others make for our growth and the sacrifices we are sometimes called to make for others. Just as God ransomed His people in *Isaiah 43*, He ransoms other people's lives for us through the trials and casualties connected to our call. The Patriarch Job understood this profound truth when he said, **"But he is unchangeable, and who can turn him back? What he desires, that he does. For he will complete what he appoints for me, and many such things are in his mind"** *(Job 23:13-14, ESV)*.

This foreword is not merely an introduction to a book—it's an invitation to reflect on how God uses every experience, every casualty, and every moment of pain in our lives to shape us into vessels for His glory. My son, Tommy, has masterfully penned a journey that weaves his life experiences with biblical truths. Through this work, he walks readers step by step—line upon line, precept upon precept—into a deeper understanding of the call and its cost.

This book reminds us that our journey has been paved by the sacrifices of others, including the ultimate sacrifice of **Jesus Christ**. Casualties are a necessary part of the process, shaping and propelling us toward fulfilling God's purposes. *Isaiah 43:3* reinforces this truth: God values His people so highly that He's willing to give nations in exchange for them. This profound truth should compel us to live with a sense of purpose, knowing that the ransom paid for us was costly but always redemptive.

As you journey through these chapters, I encourage you to open your heart to the lessons within. Let the stories and truths presented by the author challenge you to see your calling through a new lens that values the sacrifices made for you and recognizes the high calling placed on your life. Casualties are included in the call, but so is the assurance of God's presence and power to bring us and those he has ransomed through. Enjoy this transformative journey through the pages of this book. May it lead you to understand and embrace the fullness of your calling, seeing God's hand in every step along the way.

Archbishop Dr. Mark A. Wingfield-DuBois
Senior Pastor, Judah International Ministries, Mackinaw, IL

Introduction

When we think of God's call, we often envision a life filled with purpose, direction, and fulfillment. While this is true, another side to the call is usually less discussed: the adversaries we face, the struggles we endure, and the casualties we encounter. The word **casualties** refers to those harmed, lost, or impacted in the midst of a battle. In the context of our spiritual walk, it signifies the emotional, relational, and spiritual tolls that come as we pursue obedience to God's will. These moments of loss and hardship are not without purpose, but they do highlight the weight and responsibility of the calling.

"**Casualties of The Call**" reflects the reality that when God places a calling on our lives, it comes with a cost. From the biblical accounts of Aaron's sons who lost their lives for offering strange fire to the innocent children slaughtered under King Herod's decree—all because a Savior was born—these stories serve as sobering reminders of the weight of divine calling. But this book isn't just about the casualties in biblical history; it's also about the here and now. It's about you and me, the battles we face, the losses we endure, and the lives impacted by our response to God's call. Whether through delay, disobedience, or our hesitancy to embrace what God has set before us, our actions—or inactions—have ripple effects far beyond what we can see.

Throughout history and into the present day, every war or conflict has produced casualties—some expected, others unintended. In the chaos of battle, there are always those who suffer not because they were direct targets but because they were in the wrong place at the wrong time or because of decisions made by others. Consider the tragic events of **World War II**, such as the bombings of Hiroshima and Nagasaki. These actions were intended to bring a swift end to the conflict but resulted in the deaths of thousands of innocent civilians—men, women, and children simply living their lives in the targeted cities.

Fast forward to the present, conflicts like the war in Ukraine highlight this ongoing reality. Civilian areas have been targeted, displacing millions and killing countless innocent people who were simply going about their daily lives. The continuing conflict between Israel and Hamas has also seen devastating consequences, with airstrikes and ground operations within Gaza often impacting densely populated civilian areas, resulting in the loss of lives and homes for many innocent families on both sides. These examples, both past and present, underscore the devastating toll of war on those who aren't combatants but who find themselves caught in its destructive path. These unintended casualties are a sobering reminder that those who aren't directly engaged in the conflict can suffer in war. War doesn't only affect those on the front lines; it cascades out, causing devastation in the lives of those who may have never picked up a weapon or understood the reasons behind the conflict. This concept of unintended casualties is not limited to physical wars; it also applies to the spiritual battles in which we, as believers, are engaged.

The Bible clarifies we're in a spiritual war—a battle not fought with physical weapons but with spiritual ones. In **Ephesians 6:12**, the Apostle Paul writes, **"For we wrestle not against flesh and blood, but against principalities, against powers, against the rulers of the darkness of this world, against spiritual wickedness in high places."** This verse illuminates the reality that our struggles aren't merely against human adversaries but against the unseen forces of evil that seek to disrupt God's plan and purpose in our lives. There can be unintended casualties in this spiritual war, as in natural wars. These are individuals who, through no fault of their own, find themselves suffering the consequences of someone else's decisions, delays, or disobedience to God's call. Casualties may include loved ones, friends, or entire communities affected by the spiritual battles we're facing. When we delay responding to God's call, resist His leading, or step out of His will, the impact is not limited to us alone—it can affect those around us in ways we may not fully comprehend.

One of the most sobering examples of unintended casualties in the Bible is the story of David when he decided to number the people of Israel. Despite the warnings from his commander, Joab, David insisted on conducting a census of the fighting men in Israel and Judah. This act, rooted in pride and lacking trust in God, brought severe consequences. In *2 Samuel 24* and *1 Chronicles 21*, God was displeased by David's decision and sent a plague upon Israel. Seventy thousand people lost their lives because of David's choice to number the people. These individuals were not directly involved in David's decision, yet they became unintended casualties of his disobedience.

The story of David numbering the people is a powerful reminder of the far-reaching consequences our actions can have, especially when we step outside of God's will. David's repentance was genuine, and he sought to make amends by building an altar to the Lord and offering sacrifices, but the lives lost couldn't be brought back. This tragic event illustrates how the actions of a leader—someone called and anointed by God—can lead to unintended casualties when pride, fear, or disobedience take precedence over trust and obedience to God. Similarly, when Jonah ran from God's call to go to Nineveh, not only did he put himself in danger, he endangered the lives of the sailors on the ship.

Only after they threw Jonah overboard the storm ceased, but not before they were all put in harm's way (**Jonah 1:1-16**). Jonah's attempt to flee from his calling had the potential to cause unintended casualties among those who were simply going about their lives. These examples illustrate a crucial point: our spiritual decisions—or lack thereof—can profoundly impact others. When God calls us to fulfill a specific purpose, the stakes are high, and the potential for unintended casualties is real. This is why it's vital to approach our calling with the utmost seriousness and a deep sense of responsibility.

As you journey through the pages of this book, you'll encounter stories of triumph and tragedy, faith and fear, obedience and resistance. But more importantly, you'll find yourself. You'll see the moments in your life where you stood at the crossroads of decisions, where the voice of God beckoned you toward a purpose greater than yourself. You'll understand the challenges you've faced, adversaries that arose against you, and the casualties you've witnessed were all part of a greater narrative. In this narrative, God's sovereignty and love are always at work amid our greatest struggles. My intention isn't to validate or refute your call but to illustrate how your calling directly correlates to some of the casualties you may have faced or will face.

Through this book, my prayer is you'll gain a deeper understanding of the spiritual battles that are waged when you answer the call of God. May you find wisdom and guidance on how to navigate your battles with faith, courage, and obedience. The spiritual war we're engaged in is real, and the rewards for winning them are eternal. The enemy is relentless in his efforts to thwart God's purposes, and he often targets those closest to us to discourage or derail us. But take heart—God is with you in every battle and has promised to carry you through every casualty to bring you to your **"expected end"** (*Jeremiah 29:11*). As you examine your life introspectively, I pray you'll be equipped with the knowledge and spiritual tools to face the challenges ahead. May you gain the strength to persevere, the wisdom to make decisions that align with God's will, and the courage to step fully into your calling. Knowing that while casualties may occur, God is sovereign and will use the unintended consequences for His glory and your ultimate good.

Let us now walk together, learning from the examples of those who have gone before us, embracing the call with all its costs, and trusting that the God who called us is faithful. He will finish the work He has begun in us, and in the end, His glory will be revealed through every trial, every victory, and, yes, through every casualty.

Welcome to the battlefield. The call has gone out. The question is—how will you respond?

CASUALTIES OF THE CALL
CHAPTER 1
THE NATURE OF THE CALL

Chapter 1: "The Nature of The Call"

The call of God is one of the most profound experiences a person can encounter. Much like the rhythms of nature, it's a force that stirs us from within, awakening something deep in our souls that we may have never realized was there. It's a moment when divinity intersects with humanity, when the eternal purpose of God breaks into our temporal existence, and we realize that our lives have a meaning and a mission far beyond anything we could have ever imagined. Just as nature responds to the seasons and the changing elements, we, too, must learn to recognize and respond to the spiritual seasons in our lives. But what exactly is "**the call**"? How do we recognize it, and what does it mean to respond to it?

Understanding The Call

At its core, God's call is an invitation to step into the purpose for which we were created. This call isn't just about doing something for God; it's about surrendering our lives to God. It's a summons to align our lives with His will, participate in His kingdom work, and reflect His character in the world. It's an awakening with who we were created to be in order to walk as He designed for us to exist.

The call is deeply personal. God doesn't call us in a generic sense; He calls us by our name. Just as He called Moses from the burning bush, saying,

"Moses, Moses" (*Exodus 3:4*), He calls each of us individually. Our call is tailored to who we are, our gifts, our experiences, and the specific purpose He has intended for our lives. It's a call that speaks to the depths of our being, resonating with the sense that we were made for something more.

The call of God can manifest in various ways. For some, it's a dramatic, life-altering moment, like Paul's encounter with Jesus on the road to Damascus (*Acts 9:3-6*). For others, it's a quiet, persistent prompting, like Samuel hearing God's voice in the middle of the night (*1 Samuel 3:1-10*). For many, it's a gradual realization where the pieces of their life begin to align in a way that points unmistakably to God's hand at work. Yet, recognizing the call often requires spiritual sensitivity. We live in a world filled with noise—distractions, ambitions, and various voices competing for our attention. We must cultivate a heart that listens for those small prompts to hear God's call. This involves spending time in prayer, immersing ourselves in Scripture, and being attentive to the ways God may be speaking to us through circumstances, other people, and the inner witness of the Holy Spirit.

It's also important to understand that God's call is not just about our lives; His call is always connected to His larger plan. When He calls us, He's inviting us to join Him in what He's already doing in the world. The call is about finding our path and joining God on His path. It's about stepping into the flow of His redemptive work, participating in ways that advance His kingdom, and becoming a vessel through which His love and truth can be revealed to others.

The Weight of The Call

The call of God carries weight. It's not something to be taken lightly or dismissed casually. When God calls, He asks us to step out of our comfort zones, leave behind what's familiar, and trust Him in ways we have never trusted Him before. This can be extremely difficult, especially when the call leads us into unknown territory or asks us to do something that seems to be beyond our abilities.

Consider the call of Abram, who later became Abraham. In *Genesis 12:1-4*, God called Abram to leave his country, his people, and his father's household and go to a land God would show him. This call required Abram to leave everything he knew and step into a completely uncertain future, except for the fact that God was leading him. Abram's response to this call set the course for the rest of his life and the history of God's people. Abram's story is one of faith in its rawest form. He was called to abandon the security of his homeland, the familiarity of his culture, and the comfort of his family ties. He was asked to forsake everything he had known and venture into a land God promised but didn't reveal it immediately.

This journey into the unknown is a powerful image of what it means to respond to God's call. It's about trusting God more than trusting our circumstances, understanding, or plans.

The weight of the call is also seen in the lives of the prophets. When Isaiah was called, he was confronted with the holiness of God and the reality of his sinfulness. In **Isaiah 6**, Isaiah saw a vision of the Lord, high and exalted, with the train of His robe filling the temple. The seraphim were calling out, *"**Holy, holy, holy is the Lord Almighty; the whole earth is full of his glory**" (Isaiah 6:3)*. Isaiah's immediate response was one of despair: *"**Woe to me!**" I cried. "**I am ruined! For I am a man of unclean lips, and I live among a people of unclean lips, and my eyes have seen the King, the Lord Almighty**" (Isaiah 6:5)*. Yet, after God purified Isaiah's lips with a burning coal from the altar, He asked, *"**Whom shall I send? And who will go for us?**"* Isaiah's response, *"**Here am I. Send me!**" (Isaiah 6:8)*, wasn't a light-hearted acceptance. It was a response born out of a profound awareness of his unworthiness, God's grace, and the gravity of the task ahead. Isaiah's calling involved carrying messages of judgment and hope to a people who would often reject him. It required him to be steadfast in the face of opposition, to speak hard truths, and to remain faithful when the fruit of his labor wasn't immediately apparent.

The weight of the call also involves the responsibility of representing God. When we respond to His call, we become His ambassadors, messengers, and hands and feet in the world. This sacred responsibility requires us to live with integrity, humility, and a constant dependence on His grace. As Paul writes in **2 Corinthians 5:20**, "**We are therefore Christ's ambassadors, as though God were making his appeal through us.**"

Responding To The Call

Responding to God's call requires faith and trust that God knows what He's doing, even when we don't fully understand it. We must step out in obedience when we can't see the whole picture. It also requires us to be willing to let go of our plans and embrace God's plans, knowing that His ways are higher than our ways (**Isaiah 55:9**).

Faith is not just intellectual assent to a set of beliefs; it's active trust in God's character and promises. Responding to the call often means stepping into the unknown, just as Abram did. It means following God's lead when it doesn't make sense from a human perspective and being willing to say **"Yes"** to God before we know all the details of what that **"Yes"** will entail.

In my life, the call of God came during a time of intense struggle and uncertainty, which I was neither prepared for nor could fully comprehend. I felt God's call during Easter weekend in 1997, a call to stop living according to the world's system and to start living for Him. Without warning, I began to experience severe anxiety attacks; I knew something had to change in my life if I was going to get better. At that time, I didn't fully understand what all the changes would be, but I knew I had to respond. Before that weekend, I remember having moments where a strong feeling of dissatisfaction with my life came over me. I wasn't feeling suicidal or depressed, but I became totally disgusted with how I was sinfully living my life. However, every sinful act and deed seemed to entrap me further, and I couldn't escape it. I internally wrestled with myself, the person I was, and who I was called to be. I longed for something different but didn't know how to escape what I had become—trapped inside myself. Although all of that was true, responding to the call wasn't easy for me to do. It required me to let go of relationships that were holding me back, change how I was living, and trust God in ways I hadn't before. One day, as I was sitting on my couch, completely exhausted from another extreme anxiety attack, I realized that I could no longer continue living as I had been. It was as though with each anxiety attack, the person who God created me to be was no longer willing to take the back seat in my life. Those anxiety attacks were my spirit man setting off an alarm to my body that it wanted out. That person, the real me, the Godkind of man, had enough, and it was time for him to come forth. The weight of God's call pressed me, and I knew that responding would mean a radical shift in every part of my life, which I knew others wouldn't understand.

Responding to the call would involve a willingness to be transformed. Remember, as I said earlier, God doesn't just call us to do something; He calls us to be transformed! This transformation begins with the renewing process and gives us the mind of Christ so we can properly represent Him. The overall process of responding to the call involves deep inner work—allowing God to reshape and mold us into who He has created us to be. This transformation process is not always comfortable by any means. It can often involve being talked about, misunderstood, and ridiculed by people you think you know. It involves facing our fears, confronting our weaknesses, and allowing God to heal the wounds that have held us back. It's about letting God strip away the cocoon of our old life that's holding us hostage from advancing into the call.

Consider the transformation of Peter. When Jesus called Peter, he was an impulsive fisherman, quick to speak and slow to understand. But Jesus saw beyond Peter's rough edges and called him to be a fisher of men (**Matthew 4:19**) and an apostle. Throughout Peter's journey with Jesus, we see moments of great faith and moments of great failure. Yet, through it all, Jesus transformed Peter into the leader He needed him to be. When we see Peter in the book of Acts, he's a bold and courageous apostle, fearlessly proclaiming the gospel and shepherding the early Church. Responding to the call is not just about where we go or what we do; it's about who we become in the process.

The Cost of The Call

Every call comes with a cost. Jesus made this clear when He said, *"If anyone would come after me, let him deny himself and take up his cross and follow me"* (*Matthew 16:24*). The call of God often requires us to give up something—whether it's our comfort, plans, careers, relationships, or sense of control. Whatever the cost, it's worth it because what we gain is far greater than anything we could lose.

The cost of the call is vividly illustrated in the lives of the disciples. When Jesus called Peter, James, and John, they left their nets and followed Him (*Matthew 4:18-22*). This wasn't a small sacrifice—they were leaving behind their livelihood, their families, and everything they had known. But they knew the call of Jesus was worth everything they were leaving behind. Jesus Himself said, *"For whoever wants to save their life will lose it, but whoever loses their life for me will find it"* (*Matthew 16:25, NIV*). For something to be considered a sacrifice, it must first have great value to you. If it doesn't, laying it down or giving it away is not a sacrifice. In **Genesis 4:3-7**, this principle is demonstrated by Cain and Abel's offerings to God. Abel brought the firstborn of his flock—the best and most valuable—while Cain brought an offering from the fruit of the ground, likely without much thought or care. God accepted Abel's offering but rejected Cain's, not because of the type of offering but because of the heart behind it. Sacrifices that lack sincerity or cost show where our priorities truly lie. Similarly, when Jesus observed people giving their offerings at the temple, He noted how the wealthy gave large amounts out of their abundance, but a poor widow gave two small coins—all she had to live on. Jesus said, *"Truly I tell you, this poor widow has put more into the treasury than all the others"* (**Mark 12:43, NIV**). Her offering had great value because it came from her heart and cost her everything. God knows where our treasures are and desires our hearts above all. *"For where your treasure is, there will your heart be also"* (**Luke 12:34**). The sacrifices we make in obedience to His call must come from a place of true devotion and reverence, demonstrating that we value Him above all else.

For some, the cost of the call may involve persecution, rejection, or hardship. The Apostle Paul experienced this firsthand. Paul was a man of great intellect and influence, a Pharisee of

Pharisees, respected in Jewish society. But his life was turned upside down when he encountered Christ on the road to Damascus. He went from being a persecutor of Christians to being one of the most persecuted Christians. Paul faced beatings, imprisonment, and death threats for the sake of the Gospel. Yet, Paul could confidently say, *"I consider that our present sufferings are not worth comparing with the glory that will be revealed in us"* (*Romans 8:18*). Paul understood that the cost of following Christ was nothing compared to the eternal reward.

The cost of the call can also be seen in the story of the rich young ruler (*Mark 10:17-22*). This young man came to Jesus, asking what he must do to inherit eternal life. Jesus, knowing his heart, told him to sell everything he had, give to the poor, and follow Him. The young man went away sad because he had great wealth; he wasn't willing to pay the cost of the call. This story serves as a sobering reminder that the call of God often challenges the very things we hold dear. It requires us to evaluate our priorities and to be willing to lay down anything that stands in the way of following Christ wholeheartedly. The cost of the call is not just about what we give up; it's also about what we gain. Jesus promised that anyone who leaves houses, brothers, sisters, father, mother, children, or fields for His sake will receive a hundred times as much and will inherit eternal life (**Matthew 19:29**). The cost of the call is always worth it because the rewards of following Christ far outweigh the sacrifices. We gain a deeper relationship with God, a greater sense of purpose, and the joy of being part of His kingdom work.

Answering The Call to Sacrifice

When God calls, He often asks for more than just our obedience—He asks for our dreams, ambitions, and the very things we once thought defined our purpose. God's call is not just about what He wants to give us but also about what He requires us to lay down. It is a divine exchange where our earthly aspirations are surrendered in order to embrace the greater, eternal purpose He has ordained for us.

I am reminded of several people I know, each of whom had promising careers before they answered God's call to ministry. One had a full-ride college scholarship to pursue his dream of becoming a heart surgeon. His passion was to bring healing to people through medical expertise, but God redirected him and asked him to become a pastor instead. Now, he still deals with the heart—but in a far greater way, ministering to the spiritual condition of people, leading them to healing and restoration in Christ.

Another person was thriving as a pharmaceutical representative. He was highly skilled, making good money, and excelling in his career. Yet, God asked him to leave it all behind to become a full-time pastor. He traded selling prescription medicine and medical devices that could heal the body for delivering the Word of God that could heal the spirit, soul, and body.

Even in my own journey, though my passion was to run my own construction company full-time, God required me for almost 25 years to work in a Fortune 500 company in various positions beneath my abilities as a living sacrifice unto Him. Instead of building buildings, He called me to build people. I had the skills, the knowledge, and the drive to construct physical structures, but God was more concerned with constructing something eternal—forming lives, shaping destinies, and helping others answer their own call. I often felt like I had to dumb myself down to do my job. God would say to me, **"Humble yourself, and in due season, I will exalt you."** During those years, I learned how to be faithful in the low places and content with whatever job God required me to do.

This pattern is nothing new. We see it all throughout the Scriptures. As mentioned before, Peter was a fisherman before Jesus called him to become a fisher of men (**Matthew 4:19**). Elisha was plowing fields when Elijah cast his mantle upon him, requiring him to leave his life behind to serve God's prophetic purpose (**1 Kings 19:19-21**). Paul, a scholar and prominent Pharisee, had his entire trajectory changed when Jesus called him to preach the Gospel to the Gentiles (**Acts 9:15-16**).

God often places abilities within us—gifts that could lead to earthly success—but then asks us to lay them down for something greater. This is the living sacrifice that is acceptable to Him. Our previous ambitions were not meaningless or wrong; instead, they were the training ground for what God truly wanted us to do. Just like Peter's fishing skills translated into evangelism, and the person who wanted to be a heart surgeon now ministers to the spiritual heart of man, God never wastes what He deposits in us. He repurposes it for His glory.

For those wrestling with God's call and questioning why He would ask you to give up what you have worked so hard to attain, remember this: Whatever we surrender to God, He transforms into something far greater than we could ever imagine. The sacrifice is real, but so is the reward. God's plans will always exceed our own, and though the sacrifice is great, the fulfillment of walking in divine purpose is incomparable.

Living Out The Call

When we respond to the call, we're called to live it out. This means continually walking in obedience, staying close to God, and allowing Him to guide our steps. It also means being faithful in the small things, knowing that God is at work when we can't see it. Living out the call often involves seasons of preparation. Just as David was anointed king but didn't immediately take the throne, we may find that God's call on our lives involves a period of waiting, growth, and preparation. During these times, it's important to stay faithful, trusting that God is preparing us for what's ahead. David spent years in the wilderness, running from King Saul before he finally became king. These years weren't wasted; they were a crucial time of preparation, where David learned to trust God's leading and to rely on God's strength rather than his own.

In my journey, there were times when I felt like I was in a season of waiting. After responding to God's call, I didn't immediately see the changes I hoped for. I knew God called me, but I didn't know to what or when it would be my season to step into it fully. There were times of doubt, times when I wondered if I misunderstood God's call or somehow failed to live it out. I watched others being ordained and seeing them set into certain ministry offices and becoming pastors of churches, yet none of those things were happening to me. But looking back now, I can see that those were times of preparation; God was doing a more deeper work within me. He was teaching, refining, and preparing me for what He had in store for me to do. It was never about them but what He had called me to do, which was different and not the appointed time to be released. I will speak more about this in Chapter 7.

Living out the call also means being willing to adapt. Sometimes, God's call may lead us in unexpected directions or require us to change course. It's essential to remain flexible, open to God's leading, and ready to follow wherever He takes us. The Apostle Paul had plans to go to specific regions to preach the Gospel, but the Holy Spirit directed him elsewhere (**Acts 16:6-10**). Paul was sensitive to God's leading and willing to change his plans to follow God's direction. This flexibility is vital to living out the call because God's ways are often different from our own, and His plans may take us on a journey we didn't anticipate.

Another aspect of living out the call is perseverance. The call of God isn't a one-time event; it's a lifelong journey. There will be times when the road is difficult, the path is unclear, or the obstacles seem insurmountable. But living out the call means continuing to move forward, trusting that God is with us every step of the way. **Hebrews 12:1-2** encourages us to "**run with perseverance the race marked out for us, fixing our eyes on Jesus, the pioneer and perfecter of faith.**"

Living out the call also involves the community. As I mentioned earlier, God calls us not just as individuals but as part of a larger body—the Church. We are called to support, bear each other's burdens, and work together to fulfill God's purposes. The early Church in Acts is a beautiful example of this. They devoted themselves to the apostles' teaching, fellowship, breaking bread, and prayer. They were united in purpose, and as a result, God added to their number daily those who were being saved (**Acts 2:42-47**).

Conclusion: Embracing The Call

The call of God is a sacred invitation to step into the purpose for which we were created. It's a call to walk with God, to participate in His kingdom work, and to reflect His glory in the world. While the call may come with challenges, costs, and uncertainties, it also comes with the promise of God's presence, peace, and power. The nature of the call isn't only about what we do but who we're becoming in Christ—a continual process of transformation that shapes us for the purpose God has set before us.

As you consider God's call on your life, remember that He who calls you is faithful. He'll equip, sustain, and fulfill His purposes through you. Respond to the call with faith, embrace the journey with trust, and live out your calling with perseverance, knowing God is with you every step of the way. Embrace the call, not as a burden but as a privilege—a divine invitation to partner with the

Creator of the universe in His redemptive work. Whether your call leads you to the mission field, workplace, family, or community, know that God's call is unique to you and perfectly designed for the gifts, passions, and experiences He has given you.

But remember, the call is just the beginning. Like a seed planted in the ground, the call must go through a process of growth and transformation before it bears fruit. The journey may involve seasons of waiting, hiddenness, and death to certain parts of ourselves, but these are the necessary stages for the seed of God's purpose to take root and flourish. Just as nature shows us that seeds must die before they can bring forth life, we must surrender to God's process, trusting He's at work, even in unseen places. In the next chapter, we will explore **"The Process of A Seed"** and discover how God's call in our lives often mirrors the life cycle of a seed—germinating in hidden places, growing through seasons of nurturing, and ultimately bearing fruit in His perfect timing. May you walk confidently in your calling, knowing you're not alone. The God who called you will walk with you, guide you, and empower you to fulfill the purpose for which you were created. As you live out your calling, may your life be a testimony to the goodness, grace, and glory of God.

As you embrace the call, prepare your heart to enter the next phase of the journey: the process of growth, refinement, and fruitfulness—"**The Process of A Seed**."

Verily, verily, I say unto you, Except a corn of wheat fall into the ground and die, it abideth alone: but if it die, it bringeth forth much fruit.

(John 12:24 KJV)

CASUALTIES OF THE CALL
CHAPTER 2
THE PROCESS OF A SEED

Chapter 2: "The Process of A Seed"

In the journey of life and the calling of God, we often find ourselves in seasons that feel like endings—moments where everything seems to fall apart. Yet, in God's divine economy, what looks like death is often the precursor to new life—just like a seed. *"The Process of A Seed"* is a powerful metaphor for understanding how God brings forth fruitfulness in our lives. Still, it's a process that involves a death, a surrendering, and a transformation that often goes unseen beneath the surface.

The Death of A Seed: A Necessary Transformation

Jesus used the analogy of a seed to describe the paradox of life through death. In **John 12:24**, He said, **"Verily, verily, I say unto you, Except a corn of wheat fall into the ground and die, it abideth alone: but if it die, it bringeth forth much fruit."** In this simple statement, Jesus reveals a profound spiritual truth: for life to emerge, death must first occur.

When a seed is planted, it's buried in the soil, completely enveloped by the earth. From the outside, it appears as though the seed has been lost, buried, and forgotten. Yet beneath the surface, a transformation is taking place—a process called germination. As the seed's outer shell begins to break down, it undergoes death, shedding its former self. However, this death isn't the end but the beginning of a new life and growth. This process mirrors the way God works in our lives. There are seasons when we feel buried under the weight of trials, losses, or God's new way of speaking, including silence. In these moments, we might feel abandoned or forgotten, but in reality, God is working in unseen places. Just as the seed must break open to allow the life within it to emerge, we must go through a breaking process in order for God's purpose to be fully realized in us.

Surrendering to The Soil: The Place of Trust

The seed must surrender to the soil to fulfill its purpose. This surrender is an act of trust, much like our surrender to God's will. We're called to trust God knows what He's doing when we don't understand the process. Just as the seed cannot control what happens once it's buried, we, too, must relinquish control and allow God to work in us and through us in His time and His way.

My journey into understanding the process of a seed began at a young age. I was 12 years old and in the seventh grade when my father died. This was the first casualty I endured because of the call, but it definitely wasn't my last. My father's death was a moment I never imagined happening so soon, especially at my age. I wasn't prepared for it and didn't understand why it had to happen so soon. His death thrust me into a role in my home I wasn't prepared for. Although my brother was older than me, becoming the man of the house and looking after my mother and older sisters eventually fell on my shoulders.

Amazingly, the summer before my father died was the best time ever. We fished, cooked, and spent so much time together that when I found out he passed, I wasn't as overwhelmed as one might expect. It was as if our shared final experiences had been supernaturally enhanced and multiplied. Three months of hanging out felt like the equivalent of ten years. Looking back, I realized this was God's way of preparing me for the separation coming. Although I would've loved for my father to be there in my life to teach me all the things a young boy needed to learn, God had a different plan. His plan involved allowing my father to pass away and clothing me with His presence during my time of mourning. God engulfed me with His peace; my mother and siblings couldn't fully understand it. I wore peace like a ginormous thick blanket in the middle of an epic snowstorm. It was Him—His presence, comfort, and love—keeping me settled.

As I grew older, God placed other father figures in my life and took it upon Himself to teach me what I needed to know to be a man. But as God moved me from one father figure to another and as I sought out friendships, I found myself in a constant state of trying to find my identity. I began mimicking people I was around—picking up their vernacular, mannerisms, persona, and clothing style. I was searching for myself in the things of the world, but not knowing that my true identity was hidden in Christ from the beginning, which I hadn't discovered yet. This was my surrendering to the soil, trusting God would bring forth life and purpose from such a painful loss and a season of identity confusion. I had to trust God was at work, although I couldn't see it clearly or wouldn't have chosen it for myself. In **Mark 4:26-29**, Jesus tells the parable of the growing seed: *"**The kingdom of God is as if a man should scatter seed on the ground. He sleeps and rises night and day, and the seed sprouts and grows; he knows not how. The earth produces by itself, first the blade, then the ear, then the full grain in the ear.**"* This passage highlights the mystery and the patience required in the process. The farmer doesn't know how the seed grows; he simply trusts it will.

We must become content with not knowing all the details of how God will work things out for our good. We plant the seed of obedience, surrendering ourselves, desires, and plans into God's hands, and then we trust Him to bring forth the growth. This requires patience and faith, especially when we don't see immediate results or understand our current conditions.

The Breaking and The Growth: Embracing The Process

The breaking of the seed's outer shell is crucial for its growth. Only after this breaking can the seed's life begin to emerge, pushing through the soil to reach the light. This mirrors the breaking that often occurs in our lives. God allows certain situations to break us, not to destroy us, but to bring forth new life and fruitfulness.

As I reflect on the death and loss of my father, I can see how it was a breaking point in my life. It was a moment where everything familiar was stripped away, and I had to rely on God in a way I had never done before. Yet, through it all, God was preparing me for something greater. He was teaching me resilience, responsibility, and trust in His provision. In my attempts to find myself in the personas of others, God patiently guided me toward the realization that my true identity was in Him all along. The lessons I learned during that season produced fruit I couldn't have imagined then.

Consider the story of Joseph in the Bible. Joseph's life was marked by a series of events that could easily be seen as "**deaths**"—being betrayed by his brothers, sold into slavery, falsely accused, and imprisoned. Each occurrence was a breaking point where Joseph could've given up, but each "**death**" in Joseph's life was part of an extensive process that God used to bring him into his destiny. Through these trials, Joseph was transformed, and ultimately, he emerged as a leader who would save not only his family but an entire nation (**Genesis 50:20**).

In our lives, the breaking process may involve letting go of relationships, dreams, or comforts that we've held onto tightly. This means we'll probably walk through seasons of pain, uncertainty, or loss. But in the breaking, God is preparing us for something greater than we can see at the time. He's the horticulturist, cultivating the soil of our hearts so the seed of His Word and His calling can take root and produce an unscalable harvest.

Fruitfulness After The Breaking: The Fulfillment of Purpose

The ultimate goal of the seed's process is fruitfulness. Once the seed has broken and the new plant begins to grow, it moves through various stages—first, the blade; second, the ear; and finally, the full grain in the ear, as Jesus described in **Mark 4**. Each stage is essential and requires its own time of growth and development. Similarly, the fruitfulness God desires to bring forth in our lives takes time; it results from a process that cannot be rushed. Just as the seed must remain in the soil for a season before it bears fruit, we, too, must be patient as God works in us. **Galatians 6:9** encourages us, *"**And let us not be weary in well doing: for in due season we shall reap, if we faint not.**"*

In the end, the fruit that emerges is not just for our benefit but for the glory of God and the nourishment of others. The seed that falls into the ground and dies produces fruit **"after its kind,"** meaning it produces according to its nature. When we allow God to take us through the process of death and resurrection in our own lives, the fruit that emerges will be in line with the nature of Christ—*the fruit of the Spirit: love, joy, peace, patience, kindness, goodness, faithfulness, gentleness, and self-control (Galatians 5:22-23).* This fruit is meant to bless others, to feed and sustain them in their journeys. Just as the seed's growth leads to a plant that can bear more seeds, our fruitfulness in Christ leads to the multiplication of His life and His love in the world.

The Hidden Work of God: Transformation In The Dark

In moments of darkness, when it feels like we're buried beneath the weight of life's trials, it's easy to forget that God is still working. But just as a seed undergoes a radical transformation in the dark soil, however, God often does His greatest work in us during our darkest seasons. In these times, our faith is stretched, our character is refined, and our dependence on God is deepened.

The story of Gideon in the Bible comes to mind. Gideon was hiding in a winepress, threshing wheat, when the angel of the Lord appeared to him and called him a **"mighty man of valor"** (*Judges 6:12*). Gideon didn't see himself as mighty or courageous—he was afraid and uncertain. Yet, God saw what Gideon could become, not who he was at that moment. God was preparing Gideon to lead Israel to victory in the hidden place of his fear and doubt. Gideon's story reminds us that when we feel buried by fear or inadequacy, God sees the potential for growth and victory within us.

Emerging Into The Light: The Birth of New Life

After the seed has transformed beneath the soil, it begins to push through the earth, reaching for the light. This is a critical moment—the emergence of new life. What was once hidden now becomes visible, and the seed begins to fulfill its purpose of producing fruit.

Emerging from our seasons of hiddenness and breaking is often marked by a renewed sense of purpose and direction. It's when we begin to see the fruit of God's work in us. This emergence isn't without challenges; just as the young plant must push through the soil, we, too, must push through obstacles and opposition as we step into the light of our calling. The Apostle Paul experienced this firsthand. After his dramatic conversion on the road to Damascus, Paul spent time in Arabia, away from the public eye, before beginning his ministry (**Galatians 1:15-18**). During this time, God was preparing Paul for the immense work ahead. When Paul finally emerged, he became one of the most influential apostles, spreading the Gospel throughout the Roman Empire. His journey from hiddenness to fruitfulness shows us the importance of allowing God's timing to unfold, trusting that He knows the right moment for us to step into our calling.

Bearing Fruit: The Purpose of The Process

The ultimate goal of the seed's journey is to bear fruit, to produce something that brings life and nourishment to others. This fulfills its purpose, and it's the same for us. God doesn't take us through seasons of breaking and hiddenness without a purpose. He intends for us to bear fruit—fruit that will last and have a lasting impact on those around us. In **John 15:16**, Jesus said, **"You did not choose me, but I chose you and appointed you so that you might go and bear fruit—fruit that will last—and so that whatever you ask in my name the Father will give you."** The fruit we bear is the evidence of God's work in our lives, the tangible result of the process He has taken us through. This fruit is multifaceted. It includes the development of Christ-like character—the fruit of the Spirit that Paul describes in **Galatians 5:22-23**. It also consists of our impact on others as we live out our calling, whether through acts of service, words of encouragement, or the sharing of the Gospel. The fruit we bear is not for our benefit alone; it's meant to glorify God and bless others.

Just as a single seed can produce a plant that yields many seeds, our lives, when surrendered to God, have the potential to create a ripple effect of impact, influencing countless others for His kingdom. The process may be long and challenging, but the fruit that comes from it is worth every moment of waiting, every trial endured, and every step of faith taken.

Conclusion: Embracing The Seed's Process In Our Lives

The process of a seed teaches us profound lessons about the nature of God's work in our lives. It's a process that involves surrender, breaking, patience, and, ultimately, fruitfulness. Just as a seed must die to bring forth new life, we, too, must be willing to die to our agendas, comfort, and understanding to fulfill the calling God has placed on our lives. In the same way, the seed's transformation happens beneath the surface, away from the sight of others, so too do many of the most significant changes in our lives occur in quiet, hidden places. These are the moments when God works on our hearts, molding us into the people He has called us to be. God's doing His most profound work in these seasons of silence and isolation.

The journey of the seed is one of trust, surrender, and patience—values that are often tested in our walk with God. The seed doesn't fight the soil or resist the process; it simply allows itself to be planted, trusting that what appears to be an end is actually the beginning of something new. This is the essence of faith, the assurance that God is at work when we can't see it, that He's bringing forth life in the darkest, most challenging times. As you reflect on the seasons of your life where you have felt buried, broken, or in the dark, remember the process of a seed. Trust that God is at work in the hidden places, bringing forth something new and beautiful. Embrace the process, knowing in God's time, the fruit of your life will emerge, and it'll be abundant, nourishing, and life-giving to those around you.

God's call isn't simply about the end destination but the transformative journey along the way—the process through which He shapes us for His purposes. Much like the seed, we may have to undergo seasons of hiddenness and breaking, but in the end, we'll see the fulfillment of God's promise and purpose in our lives. The journey may be long, but the harvest is sure. Trust the process and trust the One who holds your life in His hands. As you walk through this process, know that God often chooses those who seem least likely, the

"not many" the world would overlook. In His kingdom, He calls the ordinary, the humble, and the weak. In the next chapter, ***The Call of The Not: "Be Not," "Was Not," and "Not Many,"*** we'll see how God delights in calling the unexpected, those willing to be a **"not"** in the world's eyes, to carry His light into places only they can reach. Embracing His call means releasing the need for recognition and instead being hidden like a seed, prepared to bear fruit in His perfect timing.

So, when you find yourself in the midst of the process, remember you're chosen, even if you feel unlikely. God often calls those who may feel inadequate or seem hidden or forgotten. But He sees you, and He's at work. In due season, you'll see the fruit of your calling—and perhaps, like Enoch, you too will find yourself becoming a **"was not,"** fully surrendered to God's purposes, no longer defined by the world but by Him alone.

Humble yourselves therefore under the mighty hand of God, that he may exalt you in due time:

(1 Peter 5:6 KJV)

CASUALTIES OF THE CALL
CHAPTER 3
"THE CALL OF THE NOT: "BE NOT," "WAS NOT," AND "NOT MANY"

Chapter 3: "The Call of The Not: "Be Not", "Was Not", and "Not Many"

The call of God on our lives is a journey unlike any other, drawing us into purpose that often defies our expectations. It's a call that reshapes our understanding of who we are and what we are here to do. In *Chapter 1*, we explored *"**The Nature of the Call**"* and saw that to answer God's call is to embrace His purpose above ours. *Chapter 2* led us deeper into this journey, showing us that, like a seed, our lives undergo a process of breaking, hidden growth, and eventual fruitfulness. Now, we'll explore what it means to respond to the calling of God to be a "**not**"—those willing to surrender their lives, ambitions, and identities for His purposes.

The Call of The "Be Not"

The invitation to "**be not**" is an invitation to a deeper level of surrender. It's a call to let go of our need to be seen, recognized, or validated by the world and to embrace a life hidden in God. This doesn't mean we become insignificant; instead, it means our lives become fully aligned with God's purposes, allowing us to operate in power and authority that comes not from ourselves but from Him. Paul captures this idea in **Romans 12:2** when he urges us, "***And be not conformed to this world: but be ye transformed by the renewing of your mind, that ye may prove what is that good, and*** *acceptable, and perfect, will of God."* To **"be not conformed"** is to resist the pressures of this world that seek to shape us. It's a decision to be set apart, rooted in God's identity for us rather than the shifting definitions of society. The world's values, built on achievement and recognition, contrast sharply with the call to **"be not,"** where we find security in the quiet assurance of God's presence and approval.

This call to **"be not"** runs throughout Scripture. In *Galatians 6:9*, Paul encourages us, *"And let us not be weary in well doing: for in due season we shall reap, if we faint not."* Choosing to **"be not weary"** means staying steadfast in the face of challenges and opposition. In our walk with God, there will be times when we feel weary and question whether the struggle is worth it. But **"being not weary"** is about trusting God's timing and His faithfulness to bring forth fruit from our faithfulness, just as the seed must remain in the soil and break open before it can grow.

Jesus invites us to **"be not"** troubled. In *John 14:1*, He says, *"Let not your heart be troubled: ye believe in God, believe also in me."* This call to **"be not troubled"** reminds us that as we go through the breaking and hidden seasons, we can find peace in God's faithfulness. We're not called to avoid trials but to walk through them anchored in faith, trusting that God is with us. Each **"be not"** is a reminder that while we face difficulties, our strength comes from God's presence in the journey. Jesus modeled this in His earthly ministry. Although He was the Son of God, He didn't seek fame, recognition, or worldly power. He emptied Himself, taking on the form of a servant, and was obedient to the point of death (**Philippians 2:5-8**). Jesus' life shows us what it means to "**be not**" in the eyes of the world yet to be fully aligned with God's purposes. His ultimate surrender—the cross—became the greatest victory, transforming His life and history. In the same way, when we choose to "**be not**," when we lay down our desires and plans in favor of God, we position ourselves to be used by Him in ways we could never imagine. Our lives become vessels of His grace, His power, and His glory. We, like Enoch, walk with God in such a way that our earthly existence becomes secondary to the eternal reality of His presence and purpose in our lives.

The Call of The "Was Not"

When we read about Enoch in **Genesis**, we encounter this profound phrase: *"**Enoch walked with God; and he was not, for God took him**"* (**Genesis 5:24**). Enoch's life wasn't defined by visible achievements or recorded miracles. He walked with God so closely that he "**was not.**" His life faded from earthly concerns as he became consumed by the presence and purpose of God. Enoch's story teaches us that there comes a point in our walk with God when what used to define us—our status, achievements, and struggles—becomes secondary. Walking with God is no longer about who we are but who He is in us. Like Enoch, our lives become hidden in Christ.

The journey of becoming **"was not"** echoes the transformation of a seed, which must die in the dark soil to bring forth life. Just as the seed's outer shell breaks to release new life, we, too, must let go of our attachments to the world's values and definitions. The call to be **"was not"** is a call to die to the need for validation from others and to allow God to shape us from the inside out. To be a **"was not"** is to reach a place of surrender so profound that our identity and purpose fully align with God. It's a life where our ambitions and plans fade into the background, making room for God's purposes to take center stage. This is where the world's standards no longer define us, and our lives become an offering to Him.

The Call of The "Not Many"

When God calls us to **"be not,"** He also calls us as part of the **"not many"** described by Paul in *1 Corinthians 1:26-29*. Paul says, *"For ye see your calling, brethren, how that not many wise men after the flesh, not many mighty, not many noble, are called."* This statement challenges our assumptions about who God chooses. The world often values the brightest, the strongest, and the most influential. But God often selects those the world might overlook—the humble, the seemingly unqualified, and those willing to be hidden, like a seed in the soil. They become a "**was not**" to make room for His presence in their lives. Consider the prophets, the apostles, and the ordinary men and women throughout Scripture whom God chose. They weren't the ones anyone would've expected. Moses argued with God about his calling, saying he couldn't speak well. Gideon hid from the enemy and considered himself the least in his family. Jeremiah thought he was too young to speak on God's behalf.

Jeremiah's story hits close to home for me. When God called me, I was 23 years old. I didn't see how it could be possible. Most of the pastors I knew were older men seasoned in life and ministry. I remember praying and telling God that He couldn't be calling me—I was too young and inexperienced. But as I was praying, God did something unexpected. He spoke to me through my mouth, saying, "**Jeremiah.**" At that time, I didn't know **Jeremiah** was a book in the Bible. I had to grab my Bible and find the book within the table of contents. When I read about Jeremiah's call, I saw myself in his story. Jeremiah told God the same thing I did—"**I'm too young.**" But God wasn't concerned about his age. God reassured Jeremiah, just as He reassured me, that it wasn't about what I saw in myself; it was about what He saw in me. That's the thing about God's call. It doesn't matter if we think we're too young, old, weak, or flawed. God isn't looking at what we bring to the table but what He can do through us if we trust Him.

The Unlikely Ones: A Pattern of God's Calling

The unlikely ones—the **"not many"**—are often the vessels God chooses to accomplish His purposes. Moses, who considered himself slow of speech, was called to confront Pharaoh and lead the Israelites out of Egypt (**Exodus 4:10-12**). Gideon, who described himself as the least in his family and from the weakest clan, was chosen to deliver Israel from the Midianites (**Judges 6:14-16**). Rahab, a woman with a questionable past, became part of the lineage of Christ because of her faith (**Matthew 1:5**). Again and again, God demonstrates that His calling is not based on human qualifications but on His sovereign grace and purpose. These stories illustrate that God delights in using those whom the world would least expect. The **"not many"** are chosen to confound the wisdom of the wise and show that God's power, not human ability, accomplishes His purposes. As Paul writes in **1 Corinthians 1:27-29**, *"But God hath chosen the foolish things of the world to confound the wise; and God hath chosen the weak things of the world to confound the things which are mighty; And base things of the world, and things which are despised, hath God chosen, yea, and things which are not, to bring to*

[57]

nought things that are: That no flesh should glory in his presence."

The essence of the call of the unlikely is that it's not about what we bring to the table—it's about God's glory being revealed through our weakness and insufficiency. When we're willing to **"be not"** in the sense of surrendering our ambitions, strength, and wisdom, God can work through us in ways that we could never accomplish on our own. Paul understood this deeply, which is why he said in **2 Corinthians 12:9-10**, *"But he said to me, 'My grace is sufficient for you, for my power is made perfect in weakness.' Therefore I will boast all the more gladly about my weaknesses, so that Christ's power may rest on me. That is why, for Christ's sake, I delight in weaknesses, in insults, in hardships, in persecutions, in difficulties. For when I am weak, then I am strong.*" This is the paradox of God's kingdom—our weaknesses become the platform for God's strength to be displayed. It's in our brokenness that God's glory shines the brightest because it's clear to everyone, including ourselves, that it's all Him and not us. As Paul also writes in **2 Corinthians 4:7**, *"But we have this treasure in earthen vessels, that the excellency of the power may be of God, and not of us.*" These **"earthen vessels"** refer to our fragile human bodies and lives, through which God reveals His power and glory. The treasure is His Spirit within us, showing whatever good comes from our lives is due to His presence and not our abilities.

"Not Many" Are Called, But All Are Chosen for His Glory

Paul's statement that **"not many"** of the wise, mighty, or noble are called is both a challenge and a comfort. It challenges our natural inclination to seek validation through human means—through our intelligence, strength, or social status. But it also comforts us with the knowledge that God's call is not dependent on our qualifications. It's rooted in His grace, His purpose, and His love.

We live in a world that often values the strong, the powerful, and the influential. But God's kingdom operates on a different set of principles. In His kingdom, the last shall be first, and the least shall be the greatest (**Matthew 20:16**). Those willing to humble themselves, to **"be not"** in the eyes of the world, are the very ones through whom God chooses to reveal His glory.

As you reflect on your journey, consider how God may be calling you to **"be not"** in the sense of surrendering your ambitions, strength, and wisdom to Him. Is He inviting you to step into a greater reliance in His power and His purpose? And how will your willingness to **"be not"** allow God to work through you in ways that will bring glory to His name? The call of the not—the **"be not," "was** not," and "**not many**"—is a call to surrender, to trust, and to embrace the reality that God's ways are higher than our ways. It's a call to walk with Him so closely that our lives become a reflection of His presence and His power in the world. In this divine economy, those who are "**not**" by the world's standards become the vessels through which God displays His glory. They're the "**not many**" chosen to walk a path the world cannot comprehend, much like Enoch, who walked with God and "**was not**." Their lives are testimonies to the fact that God doesn't choose the qualified but qualifies the chosen.

So, are you ready to be a "**not**" in God's kingdom? Are you ready to walk in the footsteps of Enoch, Jeremiah, Paul, and all the others who answered God's call—not because they were qualified, but because they were willing to be "**not**"? The world may not understand it, but you don't need the world's approval when you walk with God. You only need His.

Chapter 4: "The Death of Self"

The journey of answering God's call is one of transformation. As we've seen, God calls the unlikely, the humble, and those willing to become a **"not"** in the world's eyes. This willingness to **"be not"** often leads us to a place of profound surrender. But before we can fully embrace our identity in Christ, there is often a painful yet necessary process that must take place— God coming for our identity, stripping away the layers of self that we have built up over the years. I call this process *"**The Death of Self**,"* the necessary self-casualty that takes place as we respond to God's call.

To be a **"not"** is to reject the world's expectations and let go of our own. It's a process that calls us to release our ambitions, identities, and attachments and to submit fully to God's shaping hand. In this surrender, God doesn't simply redefine us; He uncovers the true identity He intended for us all along. This chapter is about what happens when God comes for our identity— not to take something away but to reveal the person we were always meant to be in Him. The layers of self we build up are often a defense against fear, rejection, or insecurity, and they sometimes become a way of seeking validation. From a young age, we begin to construct identities for ourselves, adopting behaviors, mannerisms, and values we think will help us fit in or stand out. Over time, these layers can take on a life of their own, masking our true identity in Christ. But in His mercy, God calls us to a more profound journey—a journey where these false layers are stripped away so our true selves can emerge.

The False Identities We Build

From a young age, we construct identities based on our experiences, environment, and the people around us. We may not realize it, but over time, we start to identify more with these constructed selves than with the person God created us to be.

This false identity came to a head in 1997 when I was 23. I started my first corporate job and was newly married, and it seemed like everything was falling into place on the surface. But inside, I was struggling. As I mentioned in Chapter 1, I began to suffer from intense anxiety attacks, and at the time, I couldn't understand why. I had no control over what was happening to me, and I didn't know how to make it stop. The cycle I was in seemed to have a never-ending loop. I wanted to change my life but didn't know how. I believed in God, but I was living a life of sin, completely disobedient to His word. I lived according to the world's system, wearing a worldly mask that hid my true self. The anxiety attacks were brutal and relentless, leaving me completely exhausted after each one. I remember one day, sitting on my couch at home, trying to figure out how I would live my life for God. I knew I needed to change, but I didn't know how. I felt trapped in my old ways, bound by the life I had been living, and completely unsure of how to break free. Around this time, I lost over 30 pounds and could hardly eat or sleep. I felt peace only when I read the Bible and prayed. However, the anxiety attacks kept coming, and with them came a deepening sense of despair. During this season, it became incredibly difficult for me to converse with people. The best way I can describe it is that it physically hurt to talk, so I often sat in silence, overwhelmed by the turmoil within. Mentally, my brain was fried and overloaded by everything happening to me. Combined with my fear of dying, it was a dreadful position that I found myself in. I pleaded with God for help and promised Him if he would heal me, I would tell everyone about him and change my life for the better.

One day, the phone rang. I recognized the voice on the other end of the line, although I didn't know the person well. He told me he heard I was sick and wanted to come by and see me. When he arrived at my home, I recognized him from the club I used to attend. We spoke many times when we saw each other in the club, but I never knew his name. He began to tell me that he had given his life to God and no longer went to clubs. He said God sent him to tell me something very specific:

"Faith without works is dead." That was all he said, and then he left my home. To this day, I never saw him again. After he left, it was as if a light turned on; I suddenly knew exactly what I needed to do. I got up, went to the side of my bed, knelt, and prayed. I told God that if He would remove those who were distractions from my life, I would live my life for Him. I started naming the people who I felt were keeping me in sin, asking God to remove them from my life. I'll discuss more about the effects of God's separations in Chapter 5; I want to speak more on it, but not now. The phone began to ring as I prayed, but I consciously decided not to answer it. One by one, those people stopped calling me. God physically moved some of them away from the city. I was finally free—free to live my life for Him, apart from the influences that held me back.

God's Invitation To Surrender

When God comes for our identity, He intends to bring us into our true purpose. But this often requires stripping away of the things we've clung to for security and significance. In **Matthew 16:24-25**, Jesus says, **"If anyone would come after me, let him deny himself and take up his cross and follow me. For whoever would save his life will lose it, but whoever loses his life for my sake will find it."** This invitation to deny ourselves is an invitation to let go of the false identities we've built and to trust God with the process of redefining who we are. The death of self is not about losing our individuality or becoming something we're not. It's about shedding the layers of fear, pride, and insecurity that have distorted our true selves. It's about allowing God to peel back the falsehoods to reveal the real person He created us to be—unique, loved, and purposed for His glory. For me, the anxiety I experienced was God's way of calling me to surrender. I had to confront the reality that the life I was living wasn't aligned with the identity He had for me. The process of surrender was painful—letting go of the life I had built, admitting that I wasn't in control, and trusting that God had something better for me. But it was in this surrender that I began to experience true freedom.

Consider the story of the Apostle Peter. Before he was known as Peter, he was Simon, a fisherman with a temper and a tendency to act impulsively. When Jesus called Simon to follow Him, He didn't just invite him into a new way of life; He gave him a new identity. ***"You are Simon son of John. You will be called Cephas"*** (which, when translated, is Peter) (***John 1:42***). This new name, meaning **"rock,"** symbolized the transformation that would take place in Simon's life. But before Peter could fully step into this new identity, he had to confront and let go of his old self. This process wasn't easy. It involved moments of failure and repentance, such as when Peter denied Jesus three times (***Luke***

22:54-62). But it was through these painful moments of self-confrontation and surrender that Peter became the rock upon which Christ would build His Church.

The Pain of The Process

The death of self is a painful process. It feels like losing parts of who we are, and in a way, we are. We're losing the parts of ourselves that were never meant to define us—the fears, the insecurities, the need for control, and the approval of others. This process often involves a series of events or circumstances that bring us face-to-face with the reality of our false identities.

For me, the anxiety attacks were the alarm bells, signaling that the life I was living wasn't sustainable and coming to an end. I had to face the fact that the personas I adopted weren't who God created me to be. I was tired of masquerading around as someone I wasn't, and my true self had enough. The anxiety was my soul's way of crying out for authenticity, for the freedom to live as the person God had called me to be. One of the most complex parts of this process is it often feels like a loss of identity. When God begins to strip away the false layers, we feel exposed, vulnerable, and unsure of who we are. But it's in this place of vulnerability that God can perform His greatest work. In surrendering our false selves, we find our true identity in Christ.

The Emergence of True Identity

The beautiful thing about the death of self is that it leads to the emergence of our true identity in Christ. When we let go of the things that have falsely defined us, we allow God to reveal who we truly are. This identity isn't based on what we do, what we have, or what others think of us; it's an identity rooted in who God says we are. In **2 Corinthians 5:17**, Paul writes, *"**Therefore, if anyone is in Christ, the new creation has come: The old has gone, the new is here!**"* This new creation is the result of the death of self. It's the transformation that takes place when we allow God to redefine us according to His purposes.

As God revealed my true identity, I began to see that the things I once clung to for security were less valuable than I thought. The approval of others, the need to fit in, the desire to be like someone else—all of these things paled in comparison to the joy of knowing who I was in Christ. I didn't have to strive to be someone I wasn't; I had to embrace who God created me to be. This doesn't mean the process is easy or we'll never struggle with our old selves again. But it does mean that we have a new foundation upon which to build our lives—a foundation that's secure, unshakable, and rooted in the truth of God's Word.

Living Out Our True Identity

Once we have experienced the death of self and the emergence of our true identity in Christ, we're called to live out that identity daily. This means walking in the confidence of knowing who we are in Him. It means rejecting the lies that try to pull us back into our old selves and standing firm in the truth of who God says we are. Living out our true identity also means embracing God's unique calling on our lives. Just as Peter was called to be a rock for the early Church, each of us has been given a specific role to play in God's kingdom. This role is not about striving to be something we're not but about faithfully living out the identity God has given us.

In **Ephesians 2:10**, Paul writes, **"For we are God's handiwork, created in Christ Jesus to do good works, which God prepared in advance for us to do."** Our true identity is not just about who we are; it's also about what we are called to do. As we embrace our identity in Christ, we're empowered to fulfill the good works that God has prepared for us. For me, this meant stepping into a new way of living that was no longer driven by fear, anxiety, or the need to fit into the world's mold. It meant letting go of the friends and influences that kept me bound to a life of sin and embracing the freedom that came from living for God. After that pivotal moment of prayer—when I asked God to remove the people distracting me—I witnessed a transformation in my life. Those leading me astray began to disappear from my life, either through circumstances beyond my control or because I no longer found joy in the things that once tempted me. As God stripped away the old influences, He began to surround me with new ones—people who encouraged me in my walk with Christ, spoke life and truth into my circumstances and helped me grow in my faith. This was the beginning of a new chapter in my life, where I could finally live out my true identity in Christ, free from the shackles of my past.

Walking In Freedom: The New Life In Christ

The freedom that comes from embracing our true identity in Christ is unlike anything the world can offer. It allows us to walk confidently in who God has created us to be without the need for approval from others or the fear of rejection. It's the freedom to live authentically, knowing that our worth isn't determined by our past, failures, or successes but by God's unchanging love. *Galatians 5:1* declares, *"It is for freedom that Christ has set us free. Stand firm, then, and do not let yourselves be burdened again by a yoke of slavery."* This freedom is not just a concept; it's a reality we can experience daily as we live out our true identity in Christ. This meant daily choosing to walk in the truth of who I was in Christ rather than who I had been or who others expected me to be. It meant making decisions aligned with my new identity, even when difficult. It meant trusting God to continue the work He had begun in me, knowing He was faithful to complete it.

This new life in Christ comes with challenges. There will still be moments of doubt, fear, and temptation we must resist. But the difference is, that I'm no longer walking alone. I'm no longer relying on my strength to get through the day. Instead, I'm leaning on the One who has called me, trusting He'll give me the grace and strength I need to walk in the freedom He has given me.

The Power of A New Testimony

As we embrace our true identity in Christ, our lives become a testimony to the power of God's grace and transformation. Our stories—of where we were, what we've been through, and who we've become—are powerful tools God uses to reach others.

Revelation 12:11 says, *"**They triumphed over him by the blood of the Lamb and by the word of their testimony**."* Our testimony of God's work can defeat the enemy's lies and bring hope to those still discovering their true identity. Sharing my testimony has become a way to encourage others who are struggling with the same things I once did—anxiety, fear, and the feeling of being trapped in a life that isn't truly theirs. I can speak to the freedom from surrendering to God, letting go of the old self, and embracing the new. I can testify to the fact that when God comes for your identity, it's not to take something from you but to give you something far better—your true self, created in His image, for His glory.

Conclusion: Embracing The Death of Self

Discovering our true identity in Christ isn't easy. It requires a willingness to let go of the false selves we have built up over the years and to embrace the process of surrender and transformation. But as painful as the death of self may be, it's the doorway to a life of true freedom and purpose. When God comes for our identity, He does so not to harm us but to set us free from the lies that have held us captive. He comes to strip away the layers that obscure our true selves and reveal the person He created us to be. This process may feel like death, but it leads to the abundant life Jesus promised (*John 10:10*).

As you reflect on your journey, consider the areas of your life where God may call you to let go of false identities. Trust that as you surrender these things to Him, He'll lead you into the fullness of who you are in Christ. Embrace the death of self, knowing it's through this death that you'll find true life—life that's rooted in the unshakable identity that God has given you.

CASUALTIES OF THE CALL
CHAPTER 5
THE CASUALTY OF SEPARATIONS

Chapter 5: "The Casualty of Separations"

The journey of answering God's call often leads us down paths that require unexpected sacrifices. In Chapter 4, we explored the **"death of self"**—the process of letting go of our constructed identities to embrace our true selves in Christ. But as we go deeper in our walk with God, He sometimes asks us to let go of the false identities we've built and certain relationships. This is what I call *"The Casualty of Separations."* When God calls us, it often involves a process of separation—drawing us away from the familiar, the comfortable, and those we hold dear to us.

Just as God begins to strip away the layers that have obscured our true identity, He sometimes separates us from people who, though significant in past seasons, may hinder the growth He desires for us now. This separation is not rejection or punishment but a divine distinction that sets us apart for His specific purposes. These separations can be painful for us and those we leave behind. God's call on our lives is unique, and to fulfill that calling, we must sometimes be set apart from others who aren't walking the same path. It's a sacrifice that echoes throughout Scripture, perhaps most notably in the story of Abraham.

When God called Abraham, He didn't just give him a promise of blessings; He gave him a command to leave his country, his people, and his father's household. **Genesis 12:1** states, **"The Lord had said to Abram, Go from your country, your people, and your father's household to the land I will show you."** God's first instruction to Abraham was a call to separation. Abraham was asked to leave behind the familiar—family, friends, and lifestyle. And while the Bible doesn't explicitly mention the emotional struggle of this departure, it's not hard to imagine the difficulty of leaving everything familiar for an unknown future.

The Pain of Letting Go

When God begins to call us away from certain people or influences, it's rarely a simple, painless process. The relationships we have built over the years, sometimes over a lifetime, are hard to leave behind; love, history, and gratitude are often woven into these connections. Yet, just as Abraham had to leave his kindred, we are sometimes called to move forward, leaving certain people behind. God knew in order for Abraham to become the father of many nations, he needed to leave behind the influences of his past—homeland, family, and the pagan practices of his culture. Abraham's obedience to this call was crucial. By separating him from his kindred, God established a new lineage, one that would be marked by faith and a covenant relationship with the Almighty. Through this act of separation, Abraham was distinguished from all others and became the father of the nation of

Israel, through whom all the nations of the earth would be blessed (**Genesis 12:2-3**).

During my journey, there came a point when I realized God was leading me to separate from people who were significant in my life. While moving from Houston, Texas, to Peoria, Illinois, to work for *Caterpillar Inc.* after graduating from college, several friends helped me transition and feel welcome in my new surroundings. Their support was valuable, and I was grateful for it. As I pressed deeper into my walk with God, I noticed some of the same individuals were influencing me in ways that pulled me back into my old sinful patterns and habits that didn't align with the new life I was seeking in Christ. I tried to maintain the friendships, reasoning that I could keep my distance without fully detaching. But God began to impress on my heart that in order to walk in the freedom He was calling me to, I needed to separate myself from their influence. It wasn't easy; some of these friends didn't understand my decision and felt hurt or rejected. They questioned why I suddenly seemed to be distancing myself. I struggled with guilt, knowing they played a crucial role in helping me during my transition to Peoria, Illinois. But I knew that if I didn't obey, I would remain stuck in a cycle that wouldn't lead me toward God's best for my life.

A Necessary Distance

God's call to separate is not about abandoning people in judgment or disdain; it's about prioritizing the new work He is doing within us. Sometimes, separation is the only way for God to bring about the transformation He desires in our lives. As painful as it may be, it allows us to create space for the healing, growth, and renewal He intends. When Abraham left his family, he wasn't just leaving a place—he was setting himself apart to become the father of a new nation, a people consecrated to God.

Like Abraham's journey, the call to separate often takes us into the unknown. We may not immediately see why God asks us to let go of certain people, but we trust He knows the outcome. The old influences, habits, and relationships can become weights that hold us back, preventing us from stepping into the fullness of our calling. By creating distance, God helps us grow closer to Him and uncover our true identity and purpose without interference.

The Strain of Separation on Both Sides

Separation is not only difficult for us; it can be challenging for the people from whom we part ways. Our departure may feel like a betrayal to those who have known us for years and have seen us at our worst and best. They may feel rejected or hurt, believing our commitment to God has cost them our friendship. In truth, the separation isn't about rejecting them personally but responding to God's direction for our lives.

In my experience, I saw how my decision to distance myself created tension. Some friends questioned my motives, wondering if I thought I was "**better**" than them since I was pursuing a closer walk with God. Others tried to pull me back, reminding me of our shared memories and encouraging me to return to familiar sinful routines. But deep down, I knew that holding onto these relationships would keep me bound to a life I was being called to leave behind. God had something new for me, and I had to trust Him enough to walk away when it hurt them and me.

One of the most challenging separations I experienced was during the season when I was struggling with extreme anxiety and doing my best to try and respond to the call of God. He placed a young married couple in our lives who helped my wife and me spiritually when I was at my lowest and couldn't help myself. This couple became dear friends, and God used them mightily to disciple me. They were further along in their walk with Christ, so I leaned on them quite a bit. The husband often came to our apartment, reading the Bible and praying for me when I was too weak to do it for myself. Through their friendship and hands, I received the baptism of the Holy Spirit. They were to me like Ananias was to Paul in **Acts**

9:17-19, guiding me through my darkness and helping me step into the light of God. Together, they introduced us to their church, and after a short time, my wife and I became members. We quickly became deeply involved in the church and felt we found a home where we could grow. When my brother lost his battle with cancer shortly after we joined, the pastor, who barely knew us, flew to Houston, Texas, to support us in our time of mourning. My brother was only 28 years old when he died; I will speak more in detail about this casualty in the next chapter. Our friends who introduced us to the church were there for us through every step of the grieving process. We were grateful beyond words and believed we'd found a community to walk with for years to come. This couple was the only clear picture we had from God of what it looked like to walk with him, so we respected them dearly.

God began to speak to me in dreams, revealing that it was time to leave the church. I wrestled with this deeply. We were only there for fifteen months, and the relationships we built with our friends felt like lifelines. This made no sense to me or my wife; however, I couldn't deny that God was speaking to me. My wife and I argued over this revelation for weeks, and I went back to God, asking Him to talk to my wife because she wasn't convinced that I was hearing from Him. God did just that in such a profound way that left no doubt it was Him.

One Sunday morning at 7:00 a.m., our home phone rang. When I answered, a man introduced himself as a pastor, saying I didn't know him, but he knew of us because his wife worked with me at *Caterpillar*. He explained that God spoke to him while brushing his teeth and told him to call me. He asked if my wife was awake, and when I said no, he asked if I could wake her and put him on the speakerphone so we both could hear. When we both were on the line, he said, **"God said to stop arguing about leaving the church—it's Him guiding you to do this. He wants you to take your place as the priest of your home, leading your family and teaching them His Word. God said that sometimes He has to take a plant out of its pot and replant it elsewhere so it can receive the nourishment it needs."** Hearing this, my wife agreed it was from God, and she was finally in unity with me on the decision to leave. Although this confirmation brought clarity and peace for the next step, it didn't lessen the pain of leaving behind our friends and the church who supported us deeply. This separation felt like a loss; although God made His will clear, we grieved to leave the community and friendships that were pivotal in our spiritual journey. It was a profound reminder that although God's call to separate is for our growth, the pain of letting go is real and significant. However, trusting God through this transition ultimately allowed us to grow closer to Him and move forward in our faith journey.

The Purpose Behind The Pain

The pain of separation, as hard as it may be, often serves a greater purpose. God uses these moments to strengthen our dependence on Him, deepen our understanding of His call, and refine our focus on the mission He has set before us. When we let go of relationships that hinder our growth, we say **"no"** to something and say **"yes"** to God's greater plan.

Consider the story of Jesus with His disciples. Among the twelve, Jesus had three—Peter, James, and John—who were set apart to walk with Him more closely. These three were present at some of the most significant moments in Jesus' ministry. They were the only disciples to witness the transfiguration on the mountain, where Jesus' divine glory was revealed (**Matthew 17:1-9**). This event was a powerful affirmation of Jesus' identity as the Son of God, and these three disciples were chosen to witness it. Their separation from the rest of the disciples underscores the unique roles they would play in the early Church.

Peter, known for his boldness and leadership, was often the spokesperson for the disciples. He was the first to confess Jesus as Christ, the Son of the living God (**Matthew 16:16**). Jesus affirmed Peter's revelation and declared that upon this rock, He would build His Church. Peter's distinct calling was to be a foundational leader, a role that required him to be set apart and prepared for greater responsibility.

James and John, the sons of Zebedee, also had unique callings. James would become the first of the apostles to be martyred, symbolizing the cost of discipleship and the ultimate separation from the world (**Acts 12:2**). John, on the other hand, was known as the disciple whom Jesus loved. He was entrusted with the care of Jesus' mother, Mary, after the crucifixion (**John 19:26-27**). He was later given the Revelation on the island of Patmos, where he recorded the final book of the New Testament.

The separation of Peter, James, and John wasn't a sign of favoritism but a reflection of God's distinct purposes for each of them. Their unique experiences and insights equipped them to lead, teach, and guide the early Church, fulfilling the specific roles God ordained for them. This selective separation illustrates that God sometimes draws us into greater intimacy with Him by calling us out from the crowd. It's often in these places of solitude and set-apart moments that He reveals Himself most profoundly, deepening our relationship with Him without the noise or interference of the world. We may experience loneliness and question why certain people are left behind, but in the end, these separations bring us closer to the purpose for which we are called. Just as Jesus drew closer to the Father in those moments of solitude, we're also called to lean more fully into God's presence in times of separation. It's a painful process, but this pain isn't without meaning. God uses it to create space within us for something greater—a heightened awareness of His voice, a strengthened faith, and a heart that beats in alignment with His will.

Trusting God Through The Transition

In times of separation, it's natural to feel a deep sense of loss. We may wonder if we've heard God clearly, questioning whether we've made the right choice or unintentionally hurt those we care about. But ultimately, the call to separate is about obedience and trusting that God's ways are higher than ours. Just as a gardener prunes a plant to foster stronger and healthier growth, God sometimes removes people or things from our lives, creating space for us to thrive in the environment He has prepared for us.

Isaiah 55:8-9 reminds us, ***"For my thoughts are not your thoughts, neither are your ways my ways," declares the Lord. "As the heavens are higher than the earth, so are my ways higher than your ways and my thoughts than your thoughts.***" Though painful, God's call to separation aligns with His higher perspective. In His wisdom, He sees the potential and growth from our obedience. In God's hands, what feels like an ending or a loss to us is often the beginning of a new season filled with purpose and opportunity for more profound growth. When we trust God through the transition, we surrender to His perspective and allow Him to shape our path, believing He's orchestrating every step according to His perfect plan.

A New Season of Relationships and Growth

One of the blessings that often follows a painful separation is the arrival of new relationships that encourage us in our walk with God. After we left the church and let go of certain friendships, God brought us to a new church and introduced us to new people—individuals who shared our faith, supported our growth, and helped us strengthen our commitment to living for Him. These relationships became a source of encouragement and accountability, reminding us that while God may call us to let go, He also provides us with the community we need for the journey ahead. In this new season, the support we received allowed us to grow spiritually in ways that wouldn't have been possible had we stayed in our former church.

Much like the pruning process that enables fresh growth, God's separations aren't the end but the beginning of a season where we're positioned to bear more fruit. In **John 15:2**, Jesus says, "**He cuts off every branch in me that bears no fruit, while every branch that does bear fruit he prunes so that it will be even more fruitful.**" The pruning may be painful, but it ultimately leads to greater fruitfulness. Just as a plant becomes healthier and produces more after pruning, our lives gain depth, resilience, and vitality after we allow God to prune us from unfruitful attachments. Through these new relationships and growth opportunities, God shows us that obedience to His call, though difficult, is never in vain. We find that He sustains us and blesses us beyond what we left behind, equipping us for what lies ahead with fresh strength and renewed purpose. In trusting Him through the season of separation, we learn that God is always at work, bringing us closer to His heart and preparing us to walk in greater fruitfulness.

Conclusion: Embracing The Call To Separation

The call to separation is one of the most challenging aspects of following God. It demands a willingness to let go, trust, and believe that God's plans are better than ours. It's a sacrifice that requires faith, courage, and the assurance that what God has ahead is worth the pain of what we leave behind.

As you reflect on your journey, consider the people, habits, or environments holding you back from fully embracing God's call. Trust that as you surrender these things to Him, He'll guide you on a deeper, more meaningful walk with Him. Remember that while separation may feel like a loss, it's often God's way of making room for something greater—a life fully aligned with His purpose and filled with His presence. Separation isn't about abandoning people or casting judgment; it's about aligning ourselves with God's perfect will when it means stepping away from the familiar or the comfortable. Just as a plant must be pruned to allow new growth, God's call to separation is His way of pruning us so that we can flourish in new ways and bear more fruit.

As you embrace the call to separation, know that the God who called you is faithful. He sees the whole picture and understands the purpose behind every shift, every step away, and every new path forward. Trust He'll provide all you need as you walk in obedience to Him. Ultimately, the casualty of separation is not a loss but a gain—a greater closeness with God, a clearer sense of purpose, and a life that shines with His presence and power.

CASUALTIES OF THE CALL

CHAPTER 6

A LIFE FOR A LIFE

Chapter 6: "A Life For A Life"

The journey of faith often calls for sacrifice—a laying down of life in ways that may be difficult to understand. It asks us to see beyond immediate pain and trust God's redemptive plan. As we saw in previous chapters, when a seed falls to the ground and dies, it brings forth much fruit. Life comes out of death, and God's purpose emerges through loss. This chapter explores the costly exchange often embedded in God's greater design—a life for a life—and how He sometimes allows tragic events and painful separations as precursors to His redemptive work.

The Children of Bethlehem: Sacrifice and Suffering For A Greater Purpose

One of the most tragic accounts in Scripture of this **"life for a life"** principle is seen in the children who were slaughtered under King Herod's command. Upon hearing of the birth of Jesus, Herod, feeling threatened by the prophecy of a new King of the Jews, ordered the massacre of every male child under two years old in Bethlehem and its surrounding areas. The unimaginable grief of countless mothers and fathers whose children were taken from them is captured in *Matthew 2:18*, *"A voice was heard in Ramah, weeping and great mourning, Rachel weeping for her children, and she would not be comforted, because they are not."* These innocent children were among those who, because of their tragic deaths, "**are not**." They were casualties in the wake of Christ's arrival. Their absence and their sacrifice were woven into the fabric of God's redemptive plan, their deaths a precursor to the life and salvation that Jesus would bring. In a way, the lives of these children were offered up—not by choice, but as part of the hostile environment into which Christ entered, marking the beginning of the battle for humanity's soul. God allowed this massacre to unfold, foreshadowing the suffering and sacrifice Jesus Himself would later endure to bring salvation to all. Although Jesus was spared from Herod's wrath, the tragic deaths of these children remind us that sometimes, God permits what appears to be unjust so He might bring about a greater justice in His timing. King Herod's evil acts didn't go unchecked; he met a dreadful end, ultimately judged by death. This illustrates the principle found in **Genesis**—that the "**sin of the Amorites**" is not always "**yet full**" (*Genesis 15:16*). God may allow evil to persist momentarily, not out of indifference, but as part of His sovereign plan to judge every man righteously, ensuring that He alone has the last word.

This painful truth—the reality that sometimes life requires a life—is not limited to biblical accounts. I experienced this firsthand when my brother passed away within months after I accepted my call. His passing, much like the innocent lives lost under Herod's decree, became a pivotal moment in my walk with God, and through it, I encountered the mystery of sacrifice and the transfer of legacy.

A Brother's Sacrifice: A Life That Paved The Way

I remember the time leading up to my brother's death as if it were yesterday. At that time, I turned my life over to God and was seeking His direction with renewed faith and dedication. As mentioned in the previous chapter, my wife and I found new Christian friends who introduced us to their church, which we recently joined. During a church service, the pastor shared a prophetic word with me, telling me that someone in my family who was ill would be alright and that my charitable acts, since giving my life to God, had somehow interceded on their behalf. I was overjoyed by this word and quickly called my brother to share it, hoping it would encourage him to keep fighting. But the journey was harder for him than I could understand. My brother couldn't easily receive my optimism—his suffering was immense, and he was weary. When the chemotherapy and radiation failed to stop the spread of the cancer, I held onto the belief that God would heal him. I prayed through each update and each new diagnosis, remaining in faith as the situation worsened. When my brother decided to forego a third round of chemotherapy, I completely understood watching him go through the side effects of those treatments was horrendous. However, I still believed in a miraculous turnaround.

One day, I received a phone call urging me to come home immediately if I wanted to see my brother before he passed. My family informed me that my brother was rushed to the hospital, and they didn't believe he would live much longer. My wife and I quickly arranged flights arriving that evening from Peoria, Illinois, to Houston, Texas. In my heart, I held onto hope. Before leaving Peoria, I asked our pastor to pray over some anointing oil so I could use it to pray for my brother's healing. As we entered the hospital room, I anointed my brother's body, and our family joined hands, praying and singing worship songs, asking and believing God to perform a miracle. As I prayed, I realized this choice wasn't mine to make. It was my brother's decision whether he would stay or be with Jesus. Respecting this, I led him through a prayer of repentance, forgiveness, and salvation, entrusting him to God's mercy. Shortly after, I stood there and watched as he took his last breath at 12:07 a.m., His passing marked a profound moment of surrender and loss, and yet, there was a familiar peace—a peace that rested upon me when my father passed. God's peace, yet again, covered me during another casualty.

After saying goodbye, I called my pastor to let him know my brother passed, and his words brought unexpected comfort: *"We didn't lose, we didn't lose*." At that moment, I began to understand that my brother's life wasn't truly lost; it was transformed, becoming the foundation of a new purpose in my life. His legacy was transferred to me.

A Legacy Received: A Life For A Life

After arriving home at my mother's house, I couldn't sleep. After laying in bed for several hours, at 3:00 a.m., I was startled by a knock at the door. Upon opening it, I found one of my best friends standing there. He had no way of knowing I was in town or knew my brother passed away earlier that morning. So, I quickly invited him inside and started sharing with him what happened. He revealed that something told him to come by, sensing something significant had occurred. I hadn't seen him since I surrendered my life to Christ, and I was unsure of how to explain my recent transformation, especially given all the sinful things we had done together. But in expressing his condolences, I felt compelled to tell him, *"I've given my life to Jesus Christ."* To my amazement, he replied, *"Me too."* At that moment, the power of God flooded through both of us. We both felt it—an undeniable and tangible force moving from the tops of our heads to the soles of our feet. We jumped back in awe, marveling at God's transforming power. Together, we stood there, praising God for His transformation of our lives. That moment with my friend confirmed the impact my brother's life and now his death would have on others.

My brother's death became the catalyst for change, not only in me but in others who knew him. At his funeral, over thirty-two people gave their lives to Christ. The legacy he left was profound. It was as if, in his passing, he transferred a mantle to me, similar to how Elisha caught Elijah's mantle and received a double portion. From that moment forward, my life took on a depth and intensity I hadn't known before. It felt like I was living the lives of two men, empowered by my brother's legacy and God's calling. The capacity to accomplish, endure, and pursue my faith seemed multiplied, and I felt my purpose was expanded. I'll speak more about this later.

The Mystery of Sacrifice: A Divine Exchange

In Scripture, God often allows a **"life for a life"** as a divine exchange. In **John 12:24**, Jesus said, **"Very truly I tell you, unless a kernel of wheat falls to the ground and dies, it remains only a single seed. But if it dies, it produces many seeds."** This paradox of death bringing life is the cornerstone of the Gospel. Christ's death on the cross paved the way for eternal life for all who believe. His sacrifice was the ultimate life given for life, a ransom that would bring freedom, redemption, and hope to humanity.

The lives taken by Herod in his pursuit of power, my brother's passing, and the symbolic act of surrendering our will to God all point to this same principle. Out of death, life is born. Out of darkness, light emerges, and out of profound loss, God's plan unfolds in ways we could never orchestrate on our own. God could've prevented Herod's massacre, just as He could have spared my brother. But He allowed these events as part of a greater narrative in His divine wisdom. The children slain by Herod became part of a prophecy fulfilled, their absence highlighting the arrival of the Savior. My brother's passing became the means by which I found a greater understanding of the calling, one that would bear fruit in ways only God could foresee.

Catching His Mantle: Living As Two

As mentioned earlier, since my brother's death, I've often felt as though I'm living a life for both of us. In the same way that Elisha caught Elijah's mantle and received a double portion of his spirit, I felt I inherited my brother's mantle. The mantle I received has allowed me to step into a larger capacity than life, as though his spirit, strength, and purpose were somehow passed on to me. The achievements, the resilience, and the dedication I've experienced since his passing feel like they belong to two men, not just one. It's as though I'm living the life of two men, accomplishing things I never thought possible and carrying on with a strength that feels beyond me. God, in His mysterious ways, has allowed my brother's life to bear fruit in mine, producing a legacy that continues to impact others. This experience has deepened my understanding of sacrifice and the weight of legacy. In losing my brother, I gained a deeper awareness of God's purposes and a profound sense of responsibility. His death marked a significant turning point. Where I once struggled to find my identity and purpose, I felt compelled to live fully, honoring his memory and God's calling on my life. This double portion of purpose, this life lived for both of us, has been a testament to the truth that God brings forth fruit from the most unlikely soil of our greatest losses.

Conclusion: Embracing The Casualty of A Life For A Life

This **"life for a life"** principle is challenging to accept, yet it holds a profound truth. A life for a life is more than just a phrase; it's a testimony to the enduring power of sacrifice, the mystery of divine timing, and the truth that, in the hands of God, no life is wasted. The children lost under Herod's rule, the innocent lives taken before their time, my brother's passing—each instance of death and sacrifice has paved the way for a greater purpose, one that only God fully understands. Though no longer present, these lives left an indelible mark that shaped the unfolding of

God's redemptive story. We're reminded that when we cannot see it, God's plan is moving forward, often in ways that defy human understanding but infuse divine purpose.

When God calls us to follow Him, He also calls us to walk a path shaped by sacrifice and surrender. The call to embrace a life for a life is a summons to trust God's design is higher than ours when it includes suffering and loss. Each life given, each sacrifice made, and each call answered becomes a seed planted in the ground, yielding new life that carries forward His purpose. Every loss and every gift of life is intertwined with God's greater call, promising fruit that'll continue to bear His glory in ways we may not yet see. Ultimately, we may never fully comprehend why God allows certain lives to be lost or sacrifices to be made, but we trust His ways are higher than ours. The casualty of a life for a life is a mystery wrapped in God's love and wisdom, revealing a legacy of hope and redemption that flows from one generation to the next, pointing us always toward the resurrection and life that can only be found in Christ. Each response to God's call weaves into His redemptive narrative, reminding us that though the path may be steep, it ultimately leads to the fullness of life in Him.

CASUALTIES OF THE CALL

CHAPTER 7

THE SEASON OF DESCENT

Chapter 7: "The Season of Descent"

In every calling, there's a season of descent—a time when God calls us to wait, to go down before He elevates us. It's the time between hearing His call and stepping into His appointed purpose. This waiting period is not passive; it's a season filled with hidden growth, preparation, and refinement where God shapes us, tests our character, and aligns our hearts with His will.

In this chapter, we'll explore the necessity of waiting on God's timing, the dangers of moving prematurely, and the consequences of delaying our response to His call. We'll uncover the lessons that emerge in the descent through personal testimonies, biblical examples, and reflections. Most importantly, we'll learn what it truly means to occupy the place He has us in until the appointed time—trusting His timing is always perfect.

Called To Wait: The Season of Preparation

The season between the call and the commissioning is often a time of obscurity and refinement. Think of David, who was anointed as king yet waited years before he could ascend to the throne. During this waiting period, David served as a shepherd, a servant, and a fugitive. Each stage of his journey was integral to his preparation, equipping him to bear the weight of his calling when the appointed time came.

In my life, I've experienced a similar call to wait. When I first received my calling, I was eager to move forward, filled with zeal and vision. I initially assumed this meant it was time to start my church. But God had other plans. He didn't immediately open doors for that path; instead, He led me into a season of learning and growing. My journey began with teaching teenagers in Sunday School—a role I hadn't anticipated. From there, I transitioned to serving as an usher. Next, I became part of the *Levitical Order* team, a group of individuals who believed they were called by God. These roles seemed far removed from my vision for my future but were essential stepping stones. I call them qualifying assignments. Through them, I learned humility, obedience, and the value of serving in any capacity God required of me, regardless of my future destination. During these years of waiting, I began to understand the depth of the call. Some lessons came through failure, others through action, and many through observing those more mature in their walk with God. This waiting season wasn't wasted; it was the training ground for God's work ahead. When I reconsider things now, I can clearly see I wasn't prepared and didn't know it. Had I started a church, I would've indeed hurt myself, my family, and other people due to my lack of understanding and immaturity.

By the time I was ordained as an Elder in my local church, the title no longer mattered to me. I had come to a place of contentment, finding joy in simply obeying God's direction and placement. I was at peace whether He chose to use me in public ministry or behind the scenes. I learned that the calling isn't about recognition but submission to His will. Titles acknowledge God's work within you, preparing and equipping you to walk in the position He has called you to. Waiting for His appointed time allows you to embrace the role with confidence and humility, knowing that His hand guides you every step of the way.

In Chapter 2, I explained the process of a seed. Not all seeds share the same germination timeframe. Some sprout quickly, breaking through the soil in days, while others remain hidden beneath the surface for weeks, months, or even years before showing signs of life. This variation reminds us that God's timing for each calling is unique. Just as certain seeds require a prolonged period in the soil to prepare for their growth, God sometimes keeps us in seasons of waiting to refine, strengthen, and equip us for the purpose He has set before us. In these moments, it's crucial to trust the process, knowing the waiting isn't wasted—it's part of God's design to ensure that when we emerge, we're ready to flourish in His purpose. **Habakkuk 2:3** says, *"**For the vision is yet for an appointed time; but at the end it shall speak, and**"* *not lie: though it tarry, wait for it; because it will surely come, it will not tarry."* You can always recognize when it's your time because God equips you with everything you need to fulfill His purpose. When the appointed moment arrives, He'll send you—not in a state of lack or uncertainty, but fully prepared to accomplish the task at hand. God never sends us unprepared for what He's called us to do. In His perfect timing, He ensures we're ready, fully equipped, and positioned to step into His work and bring glory to His name. Waiting on Him guarantees that when the vision speaks, it'll speak with clarity and purpose, reflecting His divine preparation. Consider the story of the disciples when Jesus sent them out. In **Luke 22:35**, Jesus asked them, *"When I sent you without purse, bag, or sandals, did you lack anything?"* They replied, *"Nothing."* This exchange reveals God's provision when He sends us. The disciples were sent out seemingly unprepared by worldly standards—without money, supplies, or extra clothing—but they lacked nothing because God provided for them every step of the way. This principle remains true for us today. When God sends us, He equips us. Through skills, resources, or divine connections, He ensures we have exactly what's needed for the task. The disciples' journey teaches us that stepping out in faith when it appears we're empty-handed will never leave us lacking when we're walking in God's will. His provision is perfect, and His timing ensures we're fully ready to carry out His purpose.

Waiting isn't easy in the beginning, but you'll learn to appreciate it. Waiting requires humility, patience, and unwavering trust in God's faithfulness. But it's in the waiting that we're molded, much like clay in the hands of the potter, being shaped into vessels fit for His purpose. Through this waiting process, we learn to be faithful in the small things, which prepares us to be better stewards of the greater things He has in store for us to do. As I look back, I see the season of waiting wasn't a delay but a deliberate part of God's plan. It was the descent before the ascent, a time of preparation for something greater than I could've ever imagined. In waiting, God strengthened my character, clarified my vision, and deepened my trust in Him. And now, I can confidently say that every moment of waiting was worth it, for it brought me closer to His purpose and heart.

Occupying Until He Comes: Growing In The Place of Preparation

While the season of waiting refines us, it also challenges us to remain active and faithful in the tasks at hand. Jesus gave this instruction in **Luke 19:13**: **"Occupy until I come."** This directive isn't about passivity but stewardship—making the most of the opportunities and responsibilities entrusted to us while we await His appointed time. David's story again serves as a perfect example. While waiting for the throne, David didn't sit idle. He continued shepherding, protecting his flock from lions and bears. These private victories became the foundation for his public triumph over Goliath. David's time as a shepherd prepared him for the battlefield, where he learned to rely on God's strength and develop the courage and faith he would need as king.

In my season of waiting, I realized that God was calling me to actively grow rather than sit idle. While I didn't immediately step into God's vision, I was tasked with stewarding smaller assignments. Remember, as I said earlier, I taught teenagers in Sunday School, served as an usher, participated in the intercessory prayer team, and became a part of the *Levitical Order* group. These roles seemed insignificant compared to my vision, but they were vital training grounds for what God was preparing me to do. Throughout this season, God often told me, ***"You are exactly where I want you to be."*** Through these experiences, I learned the value of faithfulness in the small things. God used these moments to develop skills, teach humility, and instill in me the discipline of service and obedience to his word. I grew in ways I couldn't have imagined, realizing that each role equipped me for the greater work ahead. This preparation period became the foundation upon which God would later build my ministry.

The lessons learned during the season of preparation are indispensable. God uses every task, every trial, and every moment of waiting to shape us into the people He has called us to be. When we "**occupy**" faithfully, we demonstrate trust in His timing and readiness to be used in His plan. In these hidden, sometimes mundane moments, God cultivates the qualities needed for the next level of our calling. As challenging as it may be, this season of growth teaches us the importance of being diligent where we are, knowing that God is working behind the scenes to bring His purposes to fruition. When the time comes to step into the fullness of His call, we can do so with confidence, knowing we've been prepared through faithful service and unwavering trust in Him.

Stepping Out Too Soon: The Cost of Moving Ahead of God

Just as there is danger in delaying, there is equal danger in moving out prematurely. Stepping into God's calling before His appointed time can bring unforeseen casualties. I learned this firsthand when I tried to move forward without waiting for God's direction. The outcome wasn't what I'd hoped; I caused confusion and hurt to those involved. God showed me through this experience that the timing of His call is as crucial as the call itself.

I recall one day when I was walking around my bathroom, making verbal declarations. Inspired by a church elder I'd seen earlier make similar proclamations before a church service, I decided to try it myself. With conviction, I began declaring boldly, *"I declare and decree that I am a man of God. I declare and decree that I am called by God. I declare and decree that I am a son of God and have been ordained by God to be His prophet to the world."* But before I could make my next declaration, I heard the Lord interrupt me, saying, *"Wait until you have been commissioned."* The word **"commissioned"** stopped me in my tracks—I realized I didn't truly understand its meaning. Curious and convicted, I opened my Bible and reached for a dictionary. The definition struck a chord: **to be officially authorized, instructed, or empowered to carry out a specific task**. My search led me to the story of Jeremiah, who wasn't only called by God but also commissioned—set apart and authorized for his divine assignment. At that point in my life, I was confident in my calling but hadn't yet been ordained or authorized by God to serve beyond what I was doing. The Lord's correction was precise: while my calling was authentic, I needed to wait for His timing and the fulfillment of his preparation process in my life. Being called was only the beginning; commissioned required alignment with God's purpose and the humility to trust in His unfolding plan. This experience taught me a critical lesson about stepping out too soon. When the call is genuine, God determines the timing of its fulfillment. Acting prematurely can lead to confusion, unintended harm, and missed opportunities to prepare appropriately for the work ahead.

The story of Moses offers another profound example of what can happen when we move ahead of God. In **Acts 7:25**, Stephen recounts Moses' early attempt to act as Israel's deliverer: **"For he supposed that his brethren would have understood how that God by his hand would deliver them: but they understood not."** Moses assumed that his fellow Israelites would recognize his God-given role to deliver them from slavery, but his assumption led to disastrous consequences. Though he was called to be Israel's deliverer, it wasn't the season for this to occur, and he hadn't yet been commissioned. In his zeal, Moses killed an Egyptian who was mistreating an Israelite, a rash act that resulted in the Egyptian's death—a casualty born from stepping ahead of God's timing. This act not only caused the death of the Egyptian but also thrust Moses into hiding in a place of fear and exile for forty years. As I mentioned, God indeed called Moses to deliver His people, but the timing and method were entirely in His hands. Moses' premature action led to consequences that neither freed his people nor advanced God's plan. Instead, it placed Moses in a season of self-imposed separation and obscurity. His assumption and haste brought unnecessary casualties and delayed the fulfillment of God's plan. The commissioning of Moses to deliver Israel properly wouldn't occur until he had an encounter with God at the site of a bush that was burning with fire but wasn't being consumed (**Exodus 3:2-4**).

I can deeply relate to Moses' experience of self-imposed exile. In my zeal to see God move powerfully, I once told a family whose loved one was gravely ill that God would heal them. I spoke with faith and conviction, believing wholeheartedly that God would honor them. But the person passed away, leaving the family heartbroken and questioning not only my words but God's character. The weight of that moment was crushing. My good intentions and my heart's desire to see God glorified ultimately caused this family more pain than peace. Like Moses, I retreated into a season of separation—this time not from people but from my willingness to pray for anyone who was sick. I couldn't bear the thought of causing more harm to anyone else because of my faith. For years, I avoided praying for anyone unwell, afraid that my words would again lead to disappointment and disillusionment for others. It wasn't until much later that God gently encouraged me to step back into this area of ministry. He reminded me that while I'm called to pray, the results belong to Him. It was humbling to realize the power to heal wasn't absolute in my hands but in His, and obedience to God requires faith in His ability and timing. Like Moses, there was a calling for me to heal the sick and work miracles, signs, and wonders, but the fruition of that calling was in God's hands, not mine.

Moses' story and my experience underscore the danger of acting on assumption rather than waiting on God's clear direction. Zeal without wisdom can lead to destruction for us and those we're called to serve. Acting prematurely risks causing casualties—whether harm to others, missed opportunities, or delays in fulfilling the very purpose we're trying to accomplish. **Psalm 27:14** says, **"Wait on the Lord: be of good courage, and he shall strengthen thine heart: wait, I say, on the Lord."** Waiting isn't easy, but it's necessary. It keeps us aligned with God's purpose, protects us from unnecessary harm, and allows Him to work out every detail for His glory and our good. Moses ultimately fulfilled his calling, but only after God brought him back on His terms and in His time. Let us learn from Moses' early mistake—and the Lord's correction in my life—and choose to wait on the Lord, trusting His timing is always the best.

Delayed Obedience: The Cost of Waiting Too Long

On the other side of the coin lies the cost of delaying our response to God's call. When we hesitate, those God has prepared for us to reach are left waiting. The man born blind, who waited until the day Jesus was sent to heal him, exemplifies how timing impacts not only the one called but also those in need of God's touch. This man lived for years in darkness, enduring the burden of his blindness until his divine appointment with Jesus. Imagine the years he spent waiting, relying on others to dress him, guide him, and place him in position until the day Jesus came and fulfilled God's promise of healing him. His life underscores a profound truth: our obedience often carries the key to someone else's breakthrough.

The story of Jonah offers another compelling example of the high cost of delayed obedience. Jonah, a prophet of God, was called to go to Nineveh and proclaim God's message of repentance. However, instead of obeying, Jonah fled in the opposite direction, boarding a ship to Tarshish in an attempt to escape God's command. His disobedience set off a chain of events that brought consequences for himself and others. As Jonah slept, a violent storm arose, threatening the lives of everyone on board. The terrified and desperate sailors cast lots to determine who was responsible for the calamity, and the lot fell on Jonah. Jonah confessed that he was fleeing from the Lord and instructed the sailors to throw him overboard to calm the storm. Reluctantly, they obeyed, and immediately the sea grew calm. Jonah's delayed obedience put the lives of the sailors in jeopardy and brought unnecessary turmoil to those who had nothing to do with his calling (**Jonah 1:1-15**). When Jonah was thrown into the sea, God sent a great fish who swallowed him up to preserve him for the mission he called him for. Inside the belly of the great fish, Jonah spent three days and three nights reflecting on his actions. In his distress, he prayed to the Lord, acknowledging His sovereignty and expressing repentance. God, in His mercy, commanded the fish to vomit Jonah onto dry land, giving him a second chance to fulfill his calling (**Jonah 2:1-10**). This time, Jonah obeyed, traveling to Nineveh, and delivered God's message. His eventual obedience led to a citywide repentance, sparing the people of Nineveh from destruction.

Jonah's story reminds us that delayed obedience can bring unnecessary casualties. His initial refusal to follow God's command endangered the lives of the sailors, prolonged the suffering of the people of Nineveh and brought him into a place of isolation and despair. Yet it also reveals the mercy of God, who is patient with us when we falter. God's call remained on Jonah's life, and His purposes were ultimately accomplished despite Jonah's initial reluctance.

I've experienced firsthand the consequences of delayed obedience and the humility it brings. There was a time when I went on a short vacation with a close friend who was also a pastor. I intended to relax and recharge, avoiding anything spiritual during this trip. However, throughout our time together, he frequently mentioned a rash that developed on his arm. Over and over, he would say, "***I don't know where this rash came from**.*" Each time, I would nod, dismiss his concern, and change the subject. I justified my selfishness by telling myself this was my vacation and I wasn't there to minister. For three days, I ignored his plight. Finally, the Lord convicted me in a way I couldn't shake. It was as though God opened my eyes to the selfishness of my heart, showing me how I failed to act. I broke down, weeping with sorrow like rain falling from my soul. I repented sincerely, asking God to forgive me for my negligence and insensitivity. After repenting, I approached my friend, tears still in my eyes, and told him I owed him an apology. I confessed that I had been with him for three days and never thought to pray for him. He was gracious, telling me not to worry, but I insisted that I needed to pray for him. As soon as I grabbed his hand, the Lord opened my spiritual eyes. I saw letters stacked on top of each other, like a coded message. As I looked, the letters began to lift off one another and separate, forming words. I read aloud the words: *"The Law of Diminishing Return."* I didn't know what that phrase meant, so I asked my friend if it made sense to him. His eyes widened as he explained it was a financial term that he knew very well from his background in finance. He said it refers to the point where adding more to something in an effort to improve it actually causes things to worsen. I asked him if anything had been added to his life recently, something intended to make him better. He paused, then said, *"Yes, my doctor just increased my heart medication."* I immediately knew this was the cause of the rash. Together, we praised God for revealing the hidden cause of his condition and providing understanding that only He could give.

Weeks later, back home from the trip, I reflected on the experience and marveled at how God worked. But I still had one question for Him: *"Lord, why did it take three days for You to reveal this?"* His response pierced my heart: *"I didn't wait three days. You did."* Those words humbled me beyond measure. I then realized that my selfishness and unwillingness to act delayed what God was ready to do. Once again, I repented and thanked Him for His patience with me and my commitment to do better.

This experience and Jonah's story underscore the cost of delayed obedience. Our hesitation doesn't only affect us; it often affects those connected to our calling. As Jonah's delay endangered the sailors and prolonged Nineveh's suffering, my reluctance to act unnecessarily prolonged my friend's discomfort. Obedience isn't only about avoiding consequences—it's about aligning with God's timing to become a vessel through which He brings healing, deliverance, and transformation. Let Jonah's story and my testimony serve as reminders: when God prompts us to act, He's already prepared someone's heart to receive it. Delayed obedience risks casualties—both seen and unseen. But when we move in God's timing, we become instruments of His grace, fulfilling His purposes in ways that cascade far beyond our immediate understanding.

The Temptation of Haste: Avoiding The Pitfalls of Impatience

The season of descent is often marked by the temptation to act prematurely. Waiting can feel endless, and the enemy seizes the opportunity to whisper lies—convincing us that God will not move quickly enough and we need to take matters into our own hands. However, the consequences of acting in haste can be just as devastating, potentially harming those we are called to help and derailing God's plan for our lives.

In my journey, there were moments when impatience crept in, urging me to forge ahead without waiting for God's clear direction. The desire to see progress and the fear of missing opportunities sometimes became overwhelming. But each time, God reminded me of the casualties that can result from moving ahead of Him.

The story of Mephibosheth in **2 Samuel 4:4** is a sobering example of the dangers of haste. After the deaths of Saul and Jonathan, Mephibosheth's nurse, in a panic, picked him up and fled, fearing for his life. Her intentions were good—she wanted to protect him—but in her rush, she dropped him. The fall left Mephibosheth permanently lame in both of his feet. Though motivated by love, her haste resulted in a lifelong casualty for the one she sought to protect.

Similarly, the story of King Saul illustrates how acting prematurely can bring significant consequences. In **1 Samuel 13**, Saul found himself in a desperate situation: the Philistines assembled for battle, and his troops were scattering in fear. The prophet Samuel instructed Saul to wait seven days for him to arrive and offer a sacrifice to God. As the days passed and Samuel didn't appear, Saul panicked. Fearful of losing the people and eager to take control of the situation, he offered the sacrifice—a role designated only for the prophet. When Samuel arrived, he rebuked Saul, saying, *"You have done a foolish thing. You have not kept the command the Lord your God gave you"* (*1 Samuel 13:13*). Because of Saul's impatience and disobedience, God declared that his kingdom would not endure. This hasty decision cost Saul his dynasty and his standing with God. His fear of the people's reaction and his unwillingness to wait led to casualties far greater than he anticipated: the loss of God's favor, the eventual downfall of his reign, and harm to the nation of Israel.

These stories remind us that haste can lead to unintended casualties—physical, spiritual, and emotional. When we act outside of God's timing, we risk harming those we're called to serve, delaying His plans, and creating setbacks for ourselves. Mephibosheth's nurse, though well-meaning, caused lasting harm. Saul's impatience cost him his kingdom and left his people in turmoil.

The temptation of haste is not just about impatience; it's about trust. Do we trust God's timing or believe we must act in our strength to make things happen? Acting prematurely often reflects a lack of faith in God's ability to work things out according to His perfect will and timing. *Psalm 37:7* reminds us, *"Be still before the Lord and wait patiently for him."* When we choose to wait, we demonstrate our faith in His plan, acknowledging His ways are higher than ours. Though waiting can be difficult, it protects us from unnecessary casualties and ensures we remain aligned with God's purpose. By trusting in His timing, we avoid the pitfalls of impatience and step into the fullness of His call, prepared and ready to fulfill His will.

Conclusion: Embracing The Descent

As we close this chapter, it's clear the season of descent is not a detour but a deliberate and essential part of God's process for shaping us into His vessels. Every calling has its waiting season—a time when God prepares us in the hidden places for the public work He has in store. While this descent can feel isolating or discouraging, it's where the greatest transformations take place, and it also serves to protect us from the casualties that can result from moving outside of His timing.

David, Moses, the disciples, Mephibosheth, and even the man born blind all experienced the tension between the call and the fulfillment of God's purpose. Each story reminds us of the necessity of patience, obedience, and trust. When these are absent, the casualties can be profound: harm to ourselves, delays in God's plans, or unintended pain to those we are called to serve. From Mephibosheth's permanent lameness caused by his nurse's haste to the Egyptian killed by Moses' premature action to the loss of Saul's kingdom through disobedience—

each casualty highlights the cost of stepping outside of God's will.

As I've said earlier, I've witnessed the impact of delayed obedience and the wounds caused by acting prematurely. My hesitation to pray for a close friend during a time of need prolonged his suffering. My eagerness to declare my role in God's kingdom before being commissioned nearly caused me to derail the process God had for me. These moments taught me that the descent is not just about waiting—it's about protecting others and ourselves from the harm that can come when we move outside of God's purpose and timing.

The descent is a refining process, a time when God ensures we're aligned with His will, equipped for His work, and ready to step forward without causing casualties. It's where we choose to be led by Him and learn humility, trust, and the value of serving faithfully in small things. **Psalm 37:7** encourages us, **"Be still before the Lord and wait patiently for him."** This waiting is active, filled with preparation and growth, ensuring we move with God's power, provision, purpose, and backing. The casualties we see in Scripture and life are sobering reminders of the importance of staying within God's timing. Acting too soon can harm others, delay God's plans, and bring unnecessary pain. Delaying our response to God's call can prolong the struggles of those we're meant to help. But in the waiting, we're shielded from these dangers, refined for His work, and positioned to act in a way that brings life, not harm, to those around us. So, embrace the descent. Trust that God is working in ways you cannot yet see. Know that every act of obedience—whether in waiting, moving, or stepping aside—has a greater purpose than you can imagine. The descent is not the end of the journey; it's the foundation for what is to come.

When the ascent comes, you'll look back on this season and see God's hand in every detail. You'll realize that the waiting wasn't wasted, the preparation wasn't in vain, and the lessons learned were essential for the work ahead. Trust the process, trust His timing, and the God who called you is faithful to bring His work to completion.

The season of descent is a gift. Embrace it fully, knowing that in due time, God will lift you to fulfill His purpose and bring glory to His name—without the casualties that come from moving outside of His perfect plan.

Chapter 8. Casualties from Disobedience

CASUALTIES OF THE CALL
CHAPTER 8
CASUALTIES FROM DISOBEDIENCE

Chapter 8: "Casualties From Disobedience"

It's a profound privilege and a weighty responsibility when God calls us. His instructions aren't arbitrary; they're designed to lead us into His best, safeguarding our success and the well-being of those connected to our calling. The call of God isn't without standards and expectations—He requires us to be holy, as He is holy. As it's written in *1 Peter 1:15-16*, *"But just as he who called you is holy, so be holy in all you do; for it is written: Be holy, because I am holy."* Though His grace is abundant, He hasn't changed how He views sin.

In Chapter 7, we explored the season of descent—the time of preparation and refinement where God calls us to wait and grow before stepping into His appointed purpose. This season protects us from the harm caused by moving prematurely or delaying our response to His call. But while waiting aligns us with His timing, disobedience throws us out of alignment and into dangerous territory. The consequences of disobedience can be devastating, creating casualties in our lives and in the lives of those we are called to serve.

In this chapter, we'll reflect on the sobering reality of what happens when we fail to align ourselves with God's will. The stories and lessons from Scripture provide vivid examples of the cost of disobedience and the casualties that follow it. They show us that although God's grace covers our sins, the consequences of our choices still carry a profound effect. These accounts aren't just historical—they're warnings and mirrors for those called to God's purpose. They remind us that the call to holiness is as relevant today as it was for those who walked before us.

The Call Requires Obedience: The Sobering Lesson from Moses

Those called by God in extraordinary ways are not exempt from the requirement of obedience. Moses, chosen to deliver Israel from bondage in Egypt, experienced this truth firsthand. His story reveals that a calling doesn't override the need for personal holiness and faithfulness to God's instructions. After encountering God at the burning bush and accepting the mission to confront Pharaoh, Moses embarked on his journey back to Egypt. However, an unexpected and life-threatening moment arose along the way. *Exodus 4:24-26* recounts a sobering incident: *"At a lodging place on the way, the Lord met Moses and was about to kill him. But Zipporah took a flint knife, cut off her son's foreskin, and touched Moses' feet with it. 'Surely you are a bridegroom of blood to me,' she said. So the Lord let him alone"* (*NIV*). This startling event reveals that Moses almost became a casualty because of his disobedience. Although He was called to deliver

Israel, he neglected to fulfill one of God's commands regarding circumcision, the sign of His covenant with Abraham and his descendants (**Genesis 17:10-14**). By failing to circumcise his son, Moses disobeyed the covenant he was entrusted to uphold. This neglect was severe enough that God was prepared to take Moses' life, emphasizing that no calling exempts us from following His word. At this moment, Moses' wife, Zipporah, interceded and stood in the gap. She performed the circumcision, acting swiftly and decisively to align their household with God's covenant. Her obedience saved Moses' life and ensured the mission to deliver Israel could continue without delay. This event underscores the gravity of obedience in the lives of those called by God. Moses was chosen to lead the Israelites, perform signs and wonders, and communicate directly with God. Yet, his calling couldn't shield him from the consequences of disobedience. This lesson reminds us that our calling doesn't exempt us from God's standards but demands greater faithfulness.

For those called to serve, Moses' near-death experience serves as a sobering reminder that disobedience, whether intentional or through neglect, carries serious consequences. Moses almost forfeited his life and mission, demonstrating that the most anointed leaders are not above God's law. It also highlights the importance of having others who can stand in the gap when we falter. Zipporah's swift action reminds us that God often places people around us to help us stay aligned with His will. Her willingness to obey and act decisively in a crisis saved Moses from becoming a casualty of his disobedience.

Moses' story challenges us to examine our lives. Are there areas where we overlooked God's instructions, assuming that our calling compensates for our disobedience? This moment in Moses' journey is a powerful example of how God values obedience above all. It reminds us that our calling, no matter how great, doesn't exempt us from the need to walk in alignment with His word. It also warns us that disobedience, in small matters, can jeopardize the very purpose God has entrusted to us.

The Cost of Profane Worship: Nadab and Abihu Consumed

For those called to God's service, worship is not merely an act of devotion but a life of surrender, reverence, and obedience. God calls us to approach Him with clean hands and pure hearts, living lives that reflect His holiness. He sets high standards for those who minister in His name, for their actions represent Him to others. *Leviticus 11:44* reminds us of this sacred expectation: *"I am the Lord your God, and you must keep yourselves holy, because I am holy"* (*GNT*).

True worship is more than rituals or offerings; it's the posture of our hearts toward God. It requires obedience to His instructions and reverence for His presence. In **John 4:24**, Jesus declared, **"God is Spirit, and only by the power of his Spirit can people worship him as he really is"** (**GNT**). This means worship must be sincere and aligned with God's Word. Worship becomes profane when it departs from these principles, prioritizing personal desires, convenience, or carelessness over God's commands. When we fail to revere the sacredness of God's presence, we risk turning holy moments into common ones. For those called to minister before Him, the stakes are higher. The call to lead others in worship and service comes with the responsibility to model obedience and uphold the sanctity of God's name.

Among those entrusted with this sacred charge was Aaron, the first high priest of Israel. Chosen by God, Aaron stood as a mediator between the people and their Creator, bearing the weight of intercession and worship on behalf of the nation. His role was one of immense honor but also profound responsibility, requiring strict adherence to God's commands. Aaron's priesthood extended beyond himself to his sons, Nadab, Abihu, Eleazar, and Ithamar, who were appointed to assist in the holy duties. This family legacy of service highlighted the privilege and gravity of their calling. Imagine the immense joy and gratification Aaron must have felt as a father watching his sons serve alongside him in the priesthood. As the high priest, Aaron carried the weighty responsibility of ministering before God on behalf of the people. His sons were chosen to share in this sacred duty. But that joy turned to anguish when Nadab and Abihu committed a grievous act of disobedience.

In **Leviticus 10**, we learn that Nadab and Abihu offered "**strange fire**" before the Lord—an act of careless disregard for God's holy instructions. The fire they presented was unauthorized, profane, and disrespectful to the sanctity of their calling. This wasn't a minor mistake but a direct violation of the holiness God required from those who served in His presence. The consequences were immediate and severe: *"**Suddenly the Lord sent fire, and it burned them to death there in the presence of the Lord**" (**Leviticus 10:2, GNT**)*. Aaron lost not one but two of his sons in a single moment. The pain of these casualties must have been unimaginable—a grief that struck at the very core of his being. Yet Aaron, as the high priest, was commanded to restrain his outward expressions of sorrow and remain steadfast in his service to God. Moses instructed him and his remaining sons, Eleazar and Ithamar, saying, *"**Do not let your hair hang loose or tear your clothes in grief, or you will die. You must not leave the entrance of the Tent, or you will die, because you have been**"*

[125]

consecrated by the anointing oil of the Lord" (*Leviticus 10:6, GNT*). Aaron's response was pivotal, not just for himself but for the entire congregation of Israel. If Aaron had grieved publicly or abandoned his priestly duties, it could have sent a message of rebellion or doubt against God's justice. Such an act might have sown confusion and fear among the people, potentially leading them to question God's holiness and the integrity of His commands. Instead, Aaron's silent submission upheld the sanctity of the priesthood and preserved the congregation's reverence for God's presence. His obedience at this moment demonstrated a profound trust in God's righteousness amidst personal agony. As parents, none of us want to see our children suffer the consequences of their mistakes, let alone lose their lives. The story of Nadab and Abihu underscores the weight of disobedience, especially for those called to lead. It reminds us that God's call is sacred and demands our full attention and respect. Their tragic deaths serve as a warning to all who God calls: our actions matter, and the way we approach our calling must reflect the holiness of the One who called us.

For those of us who are called, there will be times in our service to God when we're commanded to withhold our grief for a greater purpose. Like Aaron, I have experienced moments when obedience required me to set aside my personal pain to fulfill a higher calling. When my brother passed away, the weight of the loss was overwhelming, yet I knew I had to be strong for my mother and siblings during the funeral. God wasn't being insensitive to my grief; He was calling me to walk in His peace and strength, showing His presence through me in that deeply painful moment. I remember standing as a pillar for my family, not because I didn't feel the pain, but because God gave me the grace to endure it for their sake. It wasn't until I returned home, away from the crowd and the weight of family responsibilities, that God whispered, "**Now**." As I hung my brother's clothes in my closet, the dam broke, and I finally grieved in His presence. The tears flowed freely, and in that sacred moment, I felt the embrace of God in a way I had never experienced before. His presence was tangible, comforting, and healing. That encounter remains etched in my memory as a testimony to God's faithfulness and the profound peace that comes from obedience in the midst of unimaginable sorrow. It reminded me that while God may call us to endure for a time, He also provides a safe place to release our pain, surrounded by His love.

Considering Aaron's story and my testimony, you must reflect on your life. Are you approaching your worship and calling with the reverence God requires? Are you willing to honor Him fully when the cost is high? Worship must flow from a place of reverence, not recklessness. Those entrusted with His work must approach their roles with humility and care, reflecting the holiness of the God they serve. May we never forget the privilege of serving God, which comes with the responsibility to honor Him in all we do.

The Danger of Deceit: Ananias and Sapphira's Costly Decisions

Those called to God's service must also live lives of truth and integrity. Our words and actions must align with the holiness of the One we represent. In **Psalm 51:6**, David declares, **"Surely you desire truth in the inner parts; you teach me wisdom in the inmost place"** (**NIV**). This scripture reveals God's standard—outward obedience and inward honesty. The call of God demands that we speak truthfully, act faithfully, and live with transparency, for anything less dishonors the One who is Truth.

Truthfulness is foundational to worship and service. Deceit undermines the very nature of our relationship with God and others. When we fail to walk in truth, we compromise the message of the Gospel, creating spiritual casualties for ourselves and those who look to us for guidance. The call to truthfulness is not merely a moral expectation but a divine requirement for those entrusted with His work.

The early church provides a powerful illustration of how God views deceit within His community. It was a time of vibrant unity and sacrificial generosity, with believers freely giving to meet the needs of others. The Spirit of God was moving mightily, and the church grew in number and faith. However, a sobering event unfolded in this holy atmosphere—a stark reminder that God's standards of holiness and truth remain unchanged.

Ananias and Sapphira, a married couple within the church, chose a path of deceit that would leave a lasting mark on the community. They sold a piece of property and brought part of the proceeds to the apostles, claiming it was the full amount. Their sin wasn't in keeping some of the money for themselves; they weren't obligated to give everything. Their sin was lying to the Holy Spirit, attempting to deceive God and the church. Through the discernment of the Holy Spirit, Peter confronted Ananias: **"Why has Satan filled your heart to lie to the Holy Spirit and to keep back for yourself part of the proceeds of the land?"** (**Acts 5:3, ESV**). Upon hearing these words, Ananias immediately fell and died. Hours later, unaware of what happened, his wife, Sapphira, repeated the same lie and met the same fate. The consequences of their deceit were swift and severe. **Acts 5:11** tells us, **"And great fear came upon the whole church and upon all who heard of these things."** Their deaths weren't only a tragic end for Ananias and Sapphira but also a sobering reminder to the entire church of the weight of God's holiness. The effects of these casualties extended beyond their immediate deaths. Their actions disrupted the unity of the early church, bringing fear and grief to the congregation and reminding them that God's presence demands reverence. Look at the effects of their deceit. The early church, which had been thriving in unity, was shaken by this sudden judgment. Trust among believers may have been tested as they wrestled with the reality of sin. The fear that gripped the church wasn't only about the consequences of lying but about the recognition that God sees beyond actions to the motives of the heart. Ananias and Sapphira's deceit left scars on their legacy and the spiritual health of their community.

This story challenges us to examine our hearts. Are we presenting an honest reflection of who we are, or are we wearing masks to appear more righteous, generous, or capable than we truly are? For those called to lead, the temptation to maintain a façade can be subtle but deadly. God's eyes are not fooled by appearances; He looks directly into our hearts. The deaths of Ananias and Sapphira underscore the truth that our calling is not about what we can pretend to be but who we truly are before God. Deceit is never a private sin; its casualties are far-reaching. It can erode trust, harm relationships, and hinder God's work in our lives and communities. The story of Ananias and Sapphira reminds us that spiritual leadership carries a weighty responsibility to walk in truth. Their decision to prioritize appearances over authenticity cost them their lives and disrupted the spiritual momentum of the early church.

I've witnessed the far-reaching consequences of deceit and seen how small compromises can snowball into bigger issues, leaving broken trust and fractured relationships in their wake. One of my hardest lessons is deceit never stays hidden. Whether uncovered by man or revealed by God, the truth always comes to light. The casualties of deceit are personal and communal, impacting those who look to us for guidance and integrity.

The call to serve God requires us to walk in truth when it's uncomfortable or humbling. True worship and service flow from a place of honesty—first with God and then with others. Ananias and Sapphira's story is a vivid reminder that God values integrity above appearances. Their tragic end urges us to examine our hearts, confront hidden motives or falsehoods, and recommit ourselves to living in alignment with God's truth. Those who are called, let us heed this sobering lesson. Let us approach God's call with a spirit of transparency and humility, remembering that our actions and motives carry eternal weight. The call to serve is a privilege and a responsibility that demands our utmost sincerity and faithfulness.

May we walk in the light of truth, knowing in doing so, we honor the One who is Truth and protect those we're called to lead from becoming spiritual casualties of our disobedience.

The Ripple Effect of Sin: King David's Catastrophic Failure

For those called by God, the weight of obedience cannot be overstated. God's commands aren't merely rules to follow but protective boundaries designed to safeguard us and those connected to our lives and ministry. The call to serve Him comes with the responsibility to live a life that reflects His holiness and honors His name. Yet, when we step outside of God's will—whether through pride, negligence, or outright rebellion—the consequences often ripple far beyond ourselves, touching our families, communities, and future generations. Scripture consistently warns against the dangers of pride and complacency for those entrusted with God's call. **Proverbs 16:18** declares, **"Pride goes before destruction, and a haughty spirit before a fall"** (**ESV**), reminding us that unchecked pride can lead to devastating consequences. Likewise, **Amos 6:1** admonishes, **"Woe to those who are at ease in Zion"** (**KJV**), cautioning against a false sense of security or indifference amid responsibility. For those called to serve, these verses serve as sobering reminders to stay humble and vigilant. Pride and spiritual complacency can dull our sensitivity to God's leading, leaving us vulnerable to temptation and sin. Without humility and a constant reliance on God, we risk personal failure and harm to those who depend on our obedience.

The life of King David, a man described as being **"after God's own heart"** (*1 Samuel 13:14*), provides a powerful and sobering example of how disobedience can lead to devastating casualties. David's sin with Bathsheba—his adultery with her and the calculated murder of her husband, Uriah—set off a chain of events that brought turmoil, heartbreak, and death to his family and kingdom. His story serves as a warning to those called by God to guard against pride, compromise, and complacency, recognizing the far-reaching consequences of sin. David's transgressions began when he chose to remain in Jerusalem during a time when kings traditionally went out to battle (*2 Samuel 11:1*). His decision to delegate his responsibility to Joab and stay behind revealed a complacency and pride that left him vulnerable to temptation. From his rooftop, David saw Bathsheba bathing and desired her, setting in motion a series of sinful decisions that would lead to lasting consequences. After committing adultery with Bathsheba and discovering she was pregnant, David attempted to cover up his sin by calling her husband, Uriah, back from the battlefield. When Uriah refused to go home and sleep with his wife,

David orchestrated his death by placing him on the front lines of battle (**2 Samuel 11:14-15**). While David may have believed his actions were hidden, they were fully exposed before God. In **2 Samuel 12**, the prophet Nathan confronted David with his sin, using a parable to reveal the gravity of his actions. David's response was immediate repentance, but the judgment God pronounced over him was severe:

"Now, therefore, the sword shall never depart from your house, because you have despised me and have taken the wife of Uriah the Hittite to be your wife. Thus says the Lord, 'Behold, I will raise up evil against you out of your own house. And I will take your wives before your eyes and give them to your neighbor, and he shall lie with your wives in the sight of this sun. For you did it secretly, but I will do this thing before all Israel and before the sun'" (**2 Samuel 12:10-12, ESV**).

The first casualty of David's sin was the child conceived with Bathsheba. Despite David's fasting and fervent prayers, the child died (**2 Samuel 12:18**). Through no fault of the child, the child's death was the result of David and Bathsheba's decisions to sin against God. David's response to the child's death was nothing short of being remarkable—he worshiped. Instead of turning away from God in bitterness, he humbled himself, acknowledging God's righteousness in judgment. This moment of worship in the face of loss reveals the depth of David's relationship with God and his understanding of God's sovereignty. But the consequences of David's sin extended far beyond the loss of the child. The **"sword"** God declared would never depart from David's house became painfully evident in the rebellion of his son Absalom (*2 Samuel 15:10-14*). Absalom's defiance included taking David's wives in full view of the nation, fulfilling Nathan's prophecy. David knew that Absalom's actions were a direct result of his disobedience. This awareness weighed heavily on David, shaping his response to Absalom's rebellion. Despite Absalom's treachery, David couldn't bring himself to harm his son. He instructed his commanders, *"**Deal gently for my sake with the young man Absalom**" (2 Samuel 18:5*). David's grief over Absalom's eventual death was profound, as he mourned not only the loss of his son but also the realization that his sin set the stage for these events. He cried out in anguish, *"**O my son Absalom, my son, my son Absalom! Would I had died instead of you, O Absalom, my son, my son!**" (2 Samuel 18:33, ESV*).

David's story resonates deeply with my own experience as a father. When my two biological daughters were very young, I received a prophetic word that stayed with me for years. While making funeral arrangements for my adopted daughter's grandmother, a man I didn't know approached me and said, *"**One of your** *daughters is in lockstep with you. If you go left, she will go left. If you go right, she will go right. But the other daughter—God says she has your nature in her. She will go out, but she will come back in.*" At the time, I didn't fully grasp the significance of his words, but as my daughters grew older, I began to see the truth of the prophecy unfold. One of my daughters mirrored my steps, walking closely in alignment with me in my walk with God. The other, however, exhibited traits of my sinful struggles. Through no fault of her own, she inherited my nature—the same tendencies I wrestled with—and as a result, she made choices that led her down ungodly paths. Like David, I was humbled by the realization that my nature contributed to the challenges my daughter faced. I understood that I couldn't change the past, but I could cover her in prayer, trusting God would fulfill His promise to bring her back in His time. It was a painful and humbling lesson, but it taught me the importance of standing in the gap for my children; just as David interceded for their child and Absalom, I chose to worship, too.

David's story and my experience remind us that the ripple effects of sin are real and far-reaching. They impact us and those we're called to lead and protect. Yet, both stories also reveal the power of God's grace and redemption. While the consequences of sin cannot be erased, God's mercy provides a way forward when we turn to

Him in repentance. For those called by God, let David's life serve as a warning and encouragement. The weight of our calling demands vigilance and humility. Our actions— whether public or private—have consequences that extend far beyond ourselves. But in our failures, God's grace is sufficient to redeem and restore. Let us strive to walk in obedience, guarding against pride and complacency and trusting God to guide us in the path of righteousness.

Lessons From Their Pain

The stories of Moses, Nadab and Abihu, Ananias and Sapphira, and David are powerful reminders of the cost of disobedience. But more importantly, they challenge us to reflect on the sacredness of our calling. Each account urges us to pause, consider the weight of our responsibilities, and ask ourselves:

- Are we approaching our calling with the reverence it deserves?

- Are we walking in integrity or presenting a false image?

- Are we neglecting our responsibilities or acting out of selfishness, pride, or fear?

These stories aren't distant historical accounts— they're mirrors, revealing the dangers of disregarding God's holiness and the ripple effects of our actions. Zipporah's quick response saves the life of the would-be deliverer, Moses. The pain felt by Aaron as he continued his priestly duties despite the loss of his sons, the shock and fear that gripped the early church after Ananias and Sapphira's deaths, and the grief that consumed David over the casualties of his sin—all these moments remind us that disobedience is not just a violation of God's law; it's a betrayal of the trust He places in us.

For me, this lesson hit home during a time when I had to confront the weight of my own decisions. While watching one of my daughters struggle with choices shaped by the nature she inherited from me, I saw firsthand how my imperfections rippled into her life. It was a humbling reminder of the generational impact of our actions and the importance of standing in the gap through prayer, intercession, and unwavering trust in God's redemptive plan. Like David, I learned while the consequences of our failures may unfold painfully, God's grace remains our anchor, enabling us to press forward with humility and hope.

Practical Lessons For Walking In Obedience

- ***Revere the sacredness of your calling***: Set aside intentional time daily to reflect on the privilege of serving God. Ask Him to search your heart and align it with His holiness.

- **Walk in truth and transparency:** Regularly examine your motives and seek accountability from trusted mentors or spiritual leaders who can help you stay aligned with God's will.

- **Guard against complacency:** Remember that pride and ease can dull your sensitivity to God's leading. Stay vigilant in prayer and actively pursue humility in your walk with Him.

- **Intercede for those you lead:** Whether in ministry, family, or community, understand that your calling includes standing in the gap for others. Cover them in prayer and live as a godly example.

Hope In Grace

The weight of God's call is heavy, but His grace is sufficient. When we fail—and we will at times—God's mercy meets us in our repentance. The stories of Moses, Aaron, David, and the early church remind us that while the consequences of disobedience are real, so is the power of restoration. Embracing the lessons of obedience not only avoids casualties but allows us to walk in God's abundant blessings and spiritual growth. When we fully embrace the weight of God's call, we walk in our strength and the power and grace of the One who equips us. His holiness becomes our guide, His mercy our comfort, and His purpose our greatest reward.

Conclusion

This chapter has explored the sobering reality of the casualties that result from disobedience, particularly for those called by God. Through the stories of Moses, Nadab and Abihu, Ananias and Sapphira, and King David, we've seen that stepping outside of God's will—whether through irreverence, deceit, or pride—leads to far-reaching consequences. These consequences often extend beyond the individual, impacting families, communities, and future generations.

Each story serves as a reminder of the sacredness of our calling and the weight of our responsibility. Moses almost became a casualty of disobedience, highlighting those called to great purposes must align fully with God's commands. Nadab and Abihu's tragic deaths underscore the importance of reverence and obedience in our worship. Ananias and Sapphira's demise highlights the danger of deceit, calling us to walk in truth and integrity before God. David's life shows how pride and complacency can open the door to sin, bringing devastating ripple effects into the lives of those we're meant to protect and lead. For those called to God's service, obedience is not merely about following rules—it's about honoring the holiness of the One who has called us.

Disobedience betrays the trust God places in us, but obedience safeguards not only our lives but also the lives of those connected to our calling.

At the heart of this chapter is a call to reflection. Are we walking in humility, integrity, and reverence before God? Are we mindful of how our actions impact those around us? And most importantly, are we guarding our hearts against the temptations of pride, complacency, and compromise? The lessons from this chapter aren't meant to condemn but to guide. They remind us that while the consequences of disobedience are real and often painful, God's grace is always available to redeem, restore, and strengthen us when we turn back to Him. Let these stories challenge us to walk in greater faithfulness, knowing our obedience honors God and brings life to those we're called to serve.

...Naked came I out of my mother's womb, and naked shall I return thither: the LORD gave, and the LORD hath taken away; blessed be the name of the LORD.

(Job 1:21 KJV)

CASUALTIES OF THE CALL

CHAPTER 9

SPIRITUAL WARFARE

Chapter 9: "Spiritual Warfare"

Throughout this book, we've explored God's call, the weight of obedience, and the consequences of disobedience. Now, we turn to an equally critical aspect of the believer's journey: the reality of spiritual warfare. As those called by God, we must recognize that our obedience and faithfulness directly oppose spiritual forces that seek to hinder God's purpose. In **Ephesians 6:12**, Paul reminds us, **"For we wrestle not against flesh and blood, but against principalities, against powers, against the rulers of the darkness of this world, against spiritual wickedness in high places."**

Behind the visible struggles we face lies an unseen enemy—Satan—who operates in darkness, orchestrating the chaos, temptations, and casualties we endure. Often, his hand is not immediately recognized, yet Scripture reveals his relentless efforts to oppose God's plans and hinder His people. Satan's strategies are subtle and destructive, seeking to exploit our weaknesses and derail our calling.

In this chapter, we'll uncover Satan's characteristics and strategies, exposing his influence in our spiritual battles. Drawing from Scripture and real-life experiences, we'll explore the casualties that arise when we underestimate or ignore the spiritual forces at work. Most importantly, we'll focus on how to arm ourselves for these battles, ensuring we remain steadfast in God's strength as we walk in our divine calling.

The Battle Against Spiritual Forces

Spiritual warfare is not a peripheral concern but a central aspect of the Christian life. When God calls us, He also equips us to face the spiritual resistance that'll inevitably arise. The enemy's goal is clear: to steal, kill, and destroy (*John 10:10*). He seeks to undermine our faith, disrupt our purpose, and destroy our testimony. In doing so, the enemy often targets the things and people we hold dear, aiming to inflict pain and sow doubt through the areas closest to our hearts. He seeks to shake our trust in God and distract us from our calling by attacking our families, relationships, or cherished dreams. The Apostle Peter warns us to be vigilant, *"Be sober-minded; be watchful. Your adversary, the devil, prowls around like a roaring lion, seeking someone to devour"* (*1 Peter 5:8, ESV*). This vivid imagery reminds us that the devil is not passive in his opposition but actively seeks opportunities to attack and devour those who are advancing God's kingdom. His tactics are cunning, his methods relentless, and his goal devastating.

The Bible offers numerous examples of spiritual battles, showing the fight isn't new. In the *Old Testament*, Daniel fasted and prayed for 21 days, seeking understanding from God, only to learn that an angel sent to him was delayed by evil spiritual forces opposing his answer (**Daniel 10:12-13**). This story reveals the reality of unseen forces working against God's plans, but it also reminds us that persistence in prayer is vital. In the New Testament, Jesus faced direct opposition from Satan during His 40 days in the wilderness (**Matthew 4:1-11**). The devil tempted Him with physical needs, pride, and power—tactics still used against believers today. Jesus' victory came through His unwavering reliance on God's Word, showing us the power of Scripture in overcoming the enemy.

Those called by God must recognize that spiritual warfare isn't a sign of failure but a confirmation of our calling. The enemy doesn't waste his efforts on those who pose no threat. If you find yourself under attack, it's likely because you're walking in obedience and advancing God's kingdom.

Examples of Spiritual Struggles

Spiritual warfare often manifests in various ways:

1. **Mental and Emotional Struggles**: Feelings of doubt, fear, and anxiety can be tactics the enemy uses to discourage us. For example, after his great victory over the prophets of Baal, Elijah fell into a deep depression and fear of Jezebel's threats (**1 Kings 19:1-4**).

2. **Conflict in Relationships**: The enemy often sows division among believers, knowing unity is essential for advancing God's kingdom. Paul warned the church to avoid giving the devil a foothold through unresolved anger (*Ephesians 4:26-27*).

3. **Physical Opposition**: Job's trials included loss, illness, and suffering. Though these appeared as natural calamities, the root cause was a spiritual confrontation between God and Satan (*Job 1-2*). We'll discuss this further in the next section.

4. **Hindrances in Ministry**: Paul spoke of being **"hindered by Satan"** in his attempts to visit the Thessalonian church (*1 Thessalonians 2:18*). Spiritual resistance often targets those advancing God's work.

I've faced moments of intense spiritual opposition, especially when stepping into new seasons of ministry. There were times when anxiety, confusion, extreme temptations, and physical obstacles seemed to block the path forward. But each struggle became an opportunity to rely more fully on God's power and provision. I'll share more about this later in this chapter.

When Spiritual Warfare Gets Physical: The Story of Job

The Book of Job offers one of the most vivid and sobering accounts of spiritual warfare in Scripture. Job, described as **"blameless and upright,"** a man who **"feared God and shunned evil"** (**Job 1:1, ESV**), became the subject of a conversation between God and Satan. Satan, the accuser, challenged Job's integrity, claiming his faithfulness was conditional, dependent on God's blessings and protection. With God's permission to test Job, Satan unleashed a calculated series of devastating attacks that stripped Job of nearly everything he held dear.

First, Job's wealth—representative of his hard work and God's provision—was obliterated in a single day. His oxen and donkeys were stolen, his servants killed, and his sheep consumed by fire from heaven (**Job 1:13-16**). This was more than a financial loss; it was an assault on Job's identity as a prosperous and respected man in his community. Each report came like waves, relentless and unyielding, driving him into a deeper pit of despair. But the worst was yet to come. A messenger arrived to deliver the most devastating news of all: Job's sons and daughters, gathered together in a house for a feast, were killed when a mighty wind caused the house to collapse (**Job 1:18-19**). The loss of a child is a parent's deepest fear, but to lose all of them in a single moment was an unspeakable tragedy. The silence that followed the news must have been deafening as Job tried to process the enormity of his grief. As if the loss of his possessions and children wasn't enough, Satan targeted Job's health. Job was afflicted with painful sores from head to toe, leaving him physically debilitated and in constant agony. He sat in ashes, scraping his sores with broken pottery, a picture of complete despair and humiliation (**Job 2:7-8**). Once a man of great wealth and influence, Job was reduced to a shadow of his former self—a broken man struggling to comprehend the weight of his suffering. Job's wife, sharing in the grief of losing their children and watching her husband suffer, became a tool in Satan's hand. Her words, **"Do you still hold fast your integrity? Curse God and die"** (**Job 2:9, ESV**), echoed Satan's accusation against Job before God. While her response may seem harsh, it reflects the depth of her anguish. Her pain mirrored Job's, and her despair left her vulnerable to the enemy's manipulation. Satan's strategy was evident: to isolate Job, dismantle his support system, and tempt him to turn away from God.

What makes Job's story more compelling is what he didn't know. Job was unaware of the heavenly conversation between God and Satan. He didn't know his suffering was part of a spiritual battle—a test of his faith and character. Job's reality was filled with unanswered questions, emotional turmoil, and physical pain, yet he chose to respond with unwavering faith. Despite his suffering, Job declared, *"The Lord gave, and the Lord has taken away; blessed be the name of the Lord"* (*Job 1:21, ESV*). And in the midst of his wife under Satan's influence, he replied, *"Shall we receive good from God, and shall we not receive evil?"* (*Job 2:10, ESV*). His faith in God's sovereignty remained unshaken as he wrestled with the incomprehensibility of his circumstances. Even more striking is the Scripture's affirmation of Job's integrity: *"In all this Job did not sin with his lips"* (*Job 2:10, ESV*). This statement underscores the depth of Job's faith and self-control. In the face of relentless suffering, he refrained from accusing God or speaking words of bitterness and despair. Job's ability to guard his tongue while wrestling with profound grief and confusion serves as a powerful example of spiritual discipline for those navigating their battles. It reminds us that in the most trying times, our words can reflect faith or doubt—and Job chose faith.

The story of Job reveals not only the reality of Satan's role in spiritual warfare but also the devastating casualties that often accompany these battles. Again, Job lost his wealth, children, health, and the support of his closest companion. He endured the judgment of his friends, who wrongly assumed his suffering resulted from hidden sin. Yet through it all, Job's integrity remained intact. His faith was tested in the furnace of affliction, but it emerged purified and strengthened. For those called by God, Job's story is a powerful reminder of the unseen spiritual forces at work behind the pain and struggles we face. The enemy's goal is not only to cause suffering but also to sever our relationship with God, to make us question His goodness and turn away in despair. Job's unwavering faith stands as a beacon for us, reminding us that when we cannot understand the reasons for our suffering, we can trust in the character of the One who holds us through it all.

The casualties of Job's spiritual battle were immense—his children, possessions, health, and sense of security. Yet his endurance shows that while Satan may cause destruction, he cannot triumph over a heart fully surrendered to God. For those called to endure spiritual warfare, Job's life encourages us to remain steadfast, trusting God's purposes are greater than the pain we face, and His faithfulness will sustain us to the end.

David's Census: The Subtlety of Satan's Influence

In **1 Chronicles 21:1**, we read, *"**Satan stood against Israel and incited David to number Israel.**"* At first glance, this act of taking a census might seem innocuous—a leader assessing the strength of his nation. But beneath the surface, this decision was fueled by pride and self-reliance. David, who once trusted God wholeheartedly, now sought to measure his military might, leaning on human strength rather than divine provision.

David's commander Joab recognized the folly in this decision and cautioned him, asking, **"Why should my Lord require this? Why should it bring guilt on Israel?"** (*1 Chronicles 21:3, ESV*). Yet, despite Joab's warning, David persisted, and the consequences were swift and severe. God's response was a devastating plague that swept through the nation, claiming the lives of **70,000 men** (*1 Chronicles 21:14*). The weight of this tragedy fell squarely on David's shoulders. This was no ordinary loss—it directly resulted from his actions. Imagine the anguish of a leader who loved his people deeply, realizing he was the cause of their suffering and death. David, a shepherd from his youth, understood the sacred responsibility of caring for the flock. He risked his life to protect sheep from lions and bears (*1 Samuel 17:34-35*). Now, as king, his **"flock"** was the nation of Israel, and yet his pride placed them in harm's way. In his grief, David cried out to God, saying, **"Was it not I who gave the command to number the people? It is I who have sinned and done great evil. But these sheep, what have they done? Please let your hand, O Lord my God, be against me and against my father's house. But do not let the plague be on your people"** (*1

Chronicles 21:17, ESV). This plea reveals David's deep anguish and his shepherd's heart—a heart that was broken not just for the loss of life but for the role he played in it. Satan's strategy was deliberate and cruel. He targeted David's pride, knowing it would lead to a decision that would bring unimaginable pain to both the king and the nation. This wasn't just an attack on David—it was an attack on Israel, God's chosen people. By inciting David to act outside of God's will, Satan succeeded in causing widespread casualties and profound sorrow.

David's journey to repentance was marked by humility and sacrifice. When God instructed him to build an altar on the threshing floor of Araunah, David insisted on paying full price, saying, *"I will not take for the Lord what is yours, nor offer burnt offerings that cost me nothing"* (*1 Chronicles 21:24, ESV*). This moment was pivotal, reflecting David's understanding of true repentance: it must cost something. Through this act of obedience, the plague was stopped, but the memory of those 70,000 lives lost would remain etched in David's heart. The story of David's census highlights the subtlety of Satan's influence. Unlike the overt attacks seen in Job's life, Satan's work here was deceptive, exploiting a seemingly small compromise. This reminds us that spiritual warfare often involves subtle temptations—pride, fear, or insecurity—that can lead to devastating consequences. The lesson is clear for those called by God: we must remain vigilant, guarding against the smallest deviations from God's commandments.

David's anguish serves as a powerful reminder of the weight of leadership and the far-reaching impact of our decisions. His pain wasn't for the loss of life but for the realization that his actions opened the door for Satan to wreak havoc. This story underscores the importance of humility, obedience, and reliance on God for those who are called. It also serves as a warning: the enemy is relentless, and his goal is not just to harm us but to destroy those entrusted to our care. Yet, in this story of loss, there is hope. David's repentance and God's mercy remind us that no failure is beyond redemption. The casualties were real; the pain was deep, but God's grace was greater. For those walking in the call, David's story is a warning and a reassurance: while the cost of disobedience is high, the power of God's forgiveness and restoration is greater.

Paul's Thorn: A Messenger of Satan and A Tool of Refinement

The Apostle Paul, a man mightily used by God and responsible for much of the New Testament, wasn't immune to the realities of spiritual warfare. In *2 Corinthians 12:7*, Paul reveals, *"To keep me from becoming conceited because of these surpassingly great revelations, there was given me a thorn in my flesh, a messenger of Satan, to torment me"* (**NIV**). This thorn was a source of ongoing pain and a reminder of his dependence on God. Though its exact nature remains a mystery, Paul described it as a **"messenger of Satan,"** underscoring the spiritual origin of this trial. The presence of this thorn raises profound questions about the interplay between God's sovereignty and Satan's schemes. While Satan intended to torment Paul, God allowed it for a redemptive purpose: to keep Paul humble and reliant on His grace. This dual reality—Satan's malice and God's higher plan—reveals the complexity of spiritual warfare. It reminds us that God's purposes are at work during pain, refining and preparing us for greater effectiveness in His kingdom.

Paul's struggle with the thorn was deeply personal. He pleaded with God three times for its removal, an act that highlights both his humanity and his vulnerability. Each time, God's response was the same: *"My grace is sufficient for you, for my power is made perfect in weakness"* (**2 Corinthians 12:9, ESV**). While Paul may have desired relief, God offered him something far greater—the strength to endure. This divine response reshaped Paul's perspective, declaring, *"Therefore I will boast all the more gladly about my weaknesses, so that Christ's power may rest on me"* (*2 Corinthians 12:9,*

NIV). The thorn in Paul's flesh teaches us that not every trial is meant to be removed or resolved in the way we expect. Sometimes, God allows specific battles to persist, using them as tools of refinement and preparation. The thorn humbled Paul, ensuring his focus remained on God's power rather than his abilities or accomplishments. For those called by God, this is a vital lesson: our strength is not in what we can do but in what God can accomplish through us, even in our weakness.

Paul's experience also illustrates the importance of enduring hardship with the mindset of a soldier. In **2 Timothy 2:3-4**, Paul writes, *"**Endure hardship as a good soldier of Jesus Christ. No one engaged in warfare entangles himself with the affairs of this life, that he may please him who enlisted him as a soldier**"* (**NKJV**). Soldiers understand the importance of discipline, focus, and commitment to their mission. Similarly, we must avoid becoming entangled in worldly distractions that can compromise our spiritual effectiveness. Paul's life demonstrated this principle as he remained steadfast in his calling despite physical challenges, opposition, and persecution. The thorn wasn't only a trial but also a revelation of God's sustaining grace. Paul's ability to endure it is a powerful example for all called to spiritual warfare. His testimony reminds us that God's grace is sufficient, even when relief doesn't come as we hope. It teaches us to trust in God's higher purposes, knowing He's working all things for our good and His glory.

Paul's Thorn and The Broader Context of Spiritual Warfare

Paul's thorn was more than a personal trial; it was part of a more significant battle against evil spiritual forces. The phrase **"messenger of Satan"** suggests an active effort by the enemy to hinder Paul's ministry and disrupt his focus. Yet, in allowing this trial, God demonstrated His supreme authority over Satan. In the story of Job, Satan could only go as far as God permitted, and his schemes were ultimately used to fulfill God's purposes. The thorn also aligns with Paul's broader understanding of spiritual warfare. In *Ephesians 6:12*, he reminds us that *"our struggle is not against flesh and blood, but against the rulers, against the authorities, against the powers of this dark world and against the spiritual forces of evil in the heavenly realms"* (**NIV**). Paul's life exemplified this struggle, facing external opposition and internal challenges like the thorn. These experiences shaped his theology and his resolve, enabling him to encourage others to stand firm in faith.

For those called, Paul's thorn is a reminder that spiritual warfare is not always about external battles—it often involves internal struggles that test our character and reliance on God. The casualties we face, whether physical suffering, relational challenges, or spiritual opposition, aren't signs of God's abandonment but opportunities to experience His sustaining grace. Paul's story challenges us to embrace a soldier's mindset, enduring hardship with perseverance and faith. It reminds us that while the battles we face may be painful, they're not without purpose. God uses the most difficult trials to refine us, draw us closer to Him, and showcase His power through our weaknesses. For those engaged in spiritual warfare, this is both a comfort and a call to remain steadfast, trusting that God's grace is sufficient for every battle.

Personal Testimony: Trusting God Amid Casualties

Spiritual warfare isn't confined to the pages of Scripture—it's a reality that continues to shape the lives of those called by God. Like Job, we face moments when life's circumstances leave us feeling stripped and vulnerable, yet it's in these moments that our faith is tested and refined. One such moment in my life came during an unexpected season of loss.

Between the birth of my second and third biological daughters, my wife and I experienced a miscarriage—a casualty in our lives that brought grief and reflection. This was an unthinkable blow, made harder by the circumstances surrounding it. Usually, I attended every doctor's visit with my wife during her pregnancies. However, on this particular occasion, I was busy at work and decided to skip the appointment, trusting everything would be fine. It was during this visit that my wife received devastating news: the baby no longer had a heartbeat. I remember the phone call vividly—her voice trembling as she asked me to come to the doctor's office immediately. Driving there, my heart was heavy with worry and disbelief. I pleaded with God, hoping against hope that the doctor made a mistake and everything would turn out okay. But upon arriving, I was told definitively that the baby had passed. The doctor explained there was no pulse and scheduled a procedure to remove the baby's remains. Those three days leading up to the procedure were some of the most sobering days of my life. I did my best to comfort my wife, but the weight of the loss was profound for both of us. It was a shared pain, an ache that lingered in every quiet moment. The morning of the procedure, I drove my wife to the outpatient surgical center; my heart was heavy, yet I was determined to trust God's plan. As we drove down the highway, my mind began to wander—not in despair, but in remembrance. I thought about how God had shown Himself faithful in our lives. I reflected on moments of divine provision, unexpected blessings, and the unshakable assurance of His presence. Overwhelmed by these thoughts, I turned to my wife and said, **"God has been so good to us."** Despite the weight of what we were facing, I couldn't help but acknowledge His goodness. At that very moment, as if to test the resolve of my faith, I noticed a piece of heavy metal flying through the air, heading directly toward our brand-new vehicle. The object struck the front of the SUV, damaging the hood and radiator. My wife, startled, asked why I didn't try to avoid the object. I explained that I had been so caught up in reflecting on God's goodness that I felt no need to stop or swerve to avoid it because I didn't feel threatened. It was as though my faith shielded me from the fear of it. I quickly pulled the car over on the side of the highway, and instead of lamenting the situation, I began to praise and worship God. I thanked Him for His protection, His mercy, and His grace. In that moment of reflection and gratitude, I realized something profound: even in the midst of loss and unexpected challenges, God's goodness remains unchanging. He's faithful, and His presence sustains us, even when we don't understand His plans.

This testimony serves as a reminder that spiritual warfare often comes disguised as life's hardships. The enemy seeks to use these moments to break our spirits, but God uses them to strengthen our faith. Just as Job chose to worship in the face of unimaginable loss, I, too, found strength in praising God amid the storm. While the pain of losing our child remains a part of my story, so does the overwhelming sense of God's faithfulness—a reminder that He walks with us through every trial, equipping us to endure and emerge stronger in Him.

The Enemy's Strategy and Our Response

Satan walks about *"as a roaring lion, seeking whom he may devour"* (*1 Peter 5:8, KJV*), aiming to disrupt our calling by attacking our faith, relationships, and obedience. Whether through the pain of loss, the enticement of pride, or the weariness of prolonged battles, his goal is always the same: to separate us from God. However, through Christ, we're equipped to resist him. As *James 4:7* promises, *"Submit yourselves, then, to God. Resist the devil, and he will flee from you"* (*NIV*).

The casualties of spiritual warfare—whether physical, emotional, or spiritual—can feel overwhelming. Yet, they also refine our faith, deepen our trust, and draw us closer to God. As soldiers in His army, we're called to endure hardship and remain focused on our mission. Paul's admonition in *2 Timothy 2:3-4* reminds us to avoid entanglement with worldly distractions, choosing instead to please the One who has enlisted us.

How To Arm Oneself Spiritually

Paul offers believers a powerful and detailed guide to spiritual preparation in **Ephesians 6:10-18**, often referred to as the Armor of God. This imagery underscores the reality of spiritual warfare and equips us with practical tools to stand firm against the schemes of the enemy. Each piece of armor represents a critical aspect of the believer's defense and offense in the spiritual battle:

1. The Belt of Truth

The belt was foundational to a soldier's armor in Paul's time, securing other pieces in place. Similarly, truth is foundational to the believer's spiritual life. Ground yourself in God's truth to counter the enemy's lies and deceptions. Jesus said, *"You shall know the truth, and the truth shall free you" (John 8:32, NKJV)*. Truth anchors us, keeping us from being swayed by false doctrines, fear, or confusion.

2. The Breastplate of Righteousness

The breastplate protects the heart and vital organs, symbolizing the importance of living a life aligned with God's Word. Righteousness is both a gift and a responsibility. We're made righteous through Christ, but we must strive to walk in obedience and integrity. This guards our spiritual hearts from the enemy's accusations and temptations.

3. The Gospel of Peace

Paul describes the readiness the gospel of peace provides as shoes for our feet. Just as a soldier's footwear provides stability and mobility, the gospel equips us to stand firm and move forward in faith. The peace of Christ, which surpasses all understanding (**Philippians 4:7**), allows us to remain steadfast in the midst of chaos and prepares us to share that peace with others.

4. The Shield of Faith

The shield of faith is designed to extinguish the fiery darts of the enemy—doubts, fears, and accusations meant to weaken our resolve. Faith is our active trust in God's promises, enabling us to deflect the enemy's attacks and stand firm. **Hebrews 11:6** reminds us, **"Without faith it is impossible to please Him, for he who comes to God must believe that He is, and that He is a rewarder of those who diligently seek Him"** (**NKJV**).

5. The Helmet of Salvation

The helmet protects the mind, symbolizing the assurance of our salvation. The enemy often targets our thoughts, sowing doubt, fear, and discouragement. By focusing on the finished work of Christ and the hope of eternal life, we guard our minds against these attacks. **Romans 12:2** encourages us to **"be transformed by the** renewing of your mind," a vital process in staying spiritually armed.

6. The Sword of The Spirit

The sword is the only offensive weapon in the armor, representing the Word of God. Jesus demonstrated the power of Scripture in resisting Satan's temptations in the wilderness (**Matthew 4:1-11**). Memorizing, meditating on, and declaring God's Word equips us to counter the enemy's lies with divine truth.

7. Prayer

While not a physical piece of armor, prayer is essential for spiritual warfare. Paul instructs believers to *"pray at all times in the Spirit, with all prayer and supplication"* (**Ephesians 6:18, ESV**). Prayer connects us to God's power, provides guidance, and strengthens our resolve. Persistent, alert, and intercessory prayer fortifies ourselves and others in the battle.

The Practical Application of Spiritual Armor

Equipping ourselves with the armor of God requires intentionality and daily discipline. Regular prayer, fasting, and meditation on Scripture are not optional—they're essential for standing firm in the face of spiritual opposition. Consider these practices:

- **Daily Devotions:** Spend time in God's Word, allowing Scripture to renew your mind and strengthen your faith. ***Psalm 119:11*** reminds us, ***"I have stored up your word in my heart, that I might not sin against you"*** **(ESV)**.

- **Persistent Prayer:** Commit to a prayer life, communicating with God about your struggles, seeking His wisdom, and interceding for others. Prayer creates a direct connection to the divine power that sustains us in the battle.

- **Fasting:** Fasting sharpens our spiritual sensitivity, aligning our will with God's and breaking the hold of distractions that entangle us.

- **Community:** Surround yourself with fellow believers who can encourage and support you. ***Ecclesiastes 4:12*** states, ***"Though one may be overpowered, two can defend themselves. A cord of three strands is not quickly broken"*** **(NIV)**. Spiritual battles aren't meant to be fought alone.

The Armor of God is not just a symbolic concept; it's a practical strategy for living out the call of God amidst spiritual warfare. Each piece reminds us of our dependence on God's strength and our responsibility to actively engage in the fight. Paul emphasizes in ***Ephesians 6:13***, ***"Therefore take up the whole armor of God, that you may be able to*** *withstand in the evil day, and having done all, to stand firm" (ESV)*. Victory in spiritual warfare isn't about escaping the battle but standing firm in the face of it, armed with the power of God. Let this armor be your daily preparation as you step into the battlefield of life, knowing that the One who calls you also equips and sustains you.

Conclusion: Living As A Victorious Warrior

Throughout this chapter, we've uncovered Satan's relentless tactics, the casualties we may face, and the tools God provides to ensure our victory. Victory in spiritual warfare is not about avoiding battles but standing firm in the midst of them. Spiritual warfare is not just a series of events—it's a reality for those called by God, and our faithfulness in the battle has eternal implications.

The story of Job revealed the depth of the enemy's cruelty, as Satan sought to destroy Job through loss, grief, and despair. Yet, even in unimaginable pain, Job held onto his faith, declaring, *"Shall we receive good from God, and shall we not receive evil?" (Job 2:10, ESV)*. Job's unwavering integrity reminds us that the enemy can touch our circumstances but cannot steal our relationship with God unless we let him. Like Job, we must choose to trust God's sovereignty, even when the reasons for our suffering remain hidden.

David's misstep in numbering Israel highlighted the subtlety of Satan's influence. Satan attacked David's heart, stirring pride and self-reliance, leading to the loss of 70,000 lives (*1 Chronicles 21:14*). The weight of this tragedy crushed David's spirit. Yet, his repentance and intercession stopped the plague, showing us the power of returning to God. For those called by God, David's story is a sobering reminder that our choices affect us and countless others. Yet, in failure, God's mercy provides a path to restoration.

Paul's thorn in the flesh, described as "**a messenger of Satan**" (*2 Corinthians 12:7*), reminds us that some battles are allowed by God to refine us. While Paul pleaded for relief, God's response was clear: "*My grace is sufficient for you, for my power is made perfect in weakness*" (*2 Corinthians 12:9, ESV*). This humbling reality teaches us that victory is not always the absence of struggle but the ability to endure with God's strength.

Every story we've examined in this chapter points to one undeniable truth: the battle belongs to the Lord (*1 Samuel 17:47*). Whether Job endures unimaginable loss, David repents after catastrophic mistakes, or Paul relies on God's strength in weakness, each reminds us that victory is secured not by our might but by God's power.

As you reflect on your spiritual battles, consider these questions:

- Are you fully armed with the armor of God?

- Are you aware of the enemy's strategies and ready to resist him?

- Are you trusting in God's strength rather than your own?

Spiritual warfare isn't easy, but it's necessary. The casualties we face are real, but so is the power of God working within us. Be encouraged: the One who calls you is faithful, and He'll equip you to overcome every challenge. The battle may be fierce, but Christ already assures victory. Stand firm, warrior, knowing that God fights for you and will complete the good work He has begun in you.

CASUALTIES OF THE CALL
CHAPTER 10
HEALING FROM THE WOUNDS

Chapter 10: "Healing From The Wounds"

Throughout this book, we have examined the lives of those who carried the weight of God's call and the casualties they endured. I've shared some of my life's most personal and intimate moments, shaping my understanding of the call. As I've said before, the call of God is indeed sacred, but it's not without its challenges and casualties. As we've explored in previous chapters, the ripple effects of disobedience, spiritual warfare, and the weight of the call often leave behind wounds—not just for us but those connected to our lives and ministry.

These wounds can manifest as broken relationships, unhealed grief, and lingering pain in the hearts of those who were collateral damage in the battles we've faced. You don't forget their names or the events, but they become blood stains on your priestly garments, which are meant to keep us in the perfect will of God. This chapter is dedicated to them. It's a call to face the aftermath of the casualties, acknowledge the pain caused by our journey, and extend the same grace and healing to others that God has given us. Whether it's family members who endured suffering alongside us, friends who felt betrayed, or ourselves as we wrestle with guilt and regret, this is the time to begin the process of healing.

Dealing With The Aftermath of Casualties

When casualties arise, those God calls, and those impacted by their journey often need healing. The weight of the call doesn't rest on the shoulders of the one called—it ripples outward, touching families, communities, and strangers. For the one called, the pain of the casualties can feel like a burden too heavy to bear. The aftermath can lead to disillusionment, grief, and deep wounds for those affected. Both groups are victims in their own right and require healing.

Casualties leave scars. They remind us of the battles we've fought and the people we've lost along the way. The story of Job reminds us that while Job's faith remained steadfast, his wife bore the weight of their shared losses. Her pain caused her to lash out, becoming a tool in Satan's strategy to tempt Job. Similarly, David's decision to number Israel led to a plague that claimed 70,000 lives. Imagine the mourning that swept through the nation—the families left without fathers, brothers, and sons. They weren't only statistics; they were people whose lives were forever changed.

It's easy to focus solely on the lessons God teaches us through our trials, but what about those who bore the brunt of our mistakes or were swept up in the aftermath of our battles? Their wounds matter. Their pain must be acknowledged. As much as we desire redemption for ourselves, we must seek it for those we've unintentionally hurt.

Acknowledging Those Who've Been Hurt

The first step in healing is to acknowledge the pain. We must be willing to confront the reality of what happened, not in condemnation but in humility and compassion. Whether it's a spouse who bore the weight of our ministry sacrifices, children who felt neglected, or friends who were hurt by our actions, healing begins with honest acknowledgment.

The aftermath of casualties is a painful reality that must be faced head-on. For the one called, the wounds often come with questions: *"Did I fail?"* *"Was this my fault?"* *"Why did this happen when I was only trying to obey God?"* These questions can lead to guilt, isolation, and even a crisis of faith. For those impacted by the casualties, the questions may be different but no less painful: *"Why did God allow this?"* *"What did I do to deserve this?"* *"How can I trust again?"* Their wounds are often compounded by the sense that they were collateral damage in someone else's journey.

The story of Job shows us that the one called and those affected by casualties need healing. Job suffered immense loss, but so did his wife. Her pain, though expressed differently, was just as real. Her outburst, *"Curse God and die"* (*Job 2:9*), reflects her anguish and disillusionment. She, too, needed healing, though her journey would look different from Job's. This reminds us that those close to the called—spouses, children, friends, congregant members—are often casualties themselves. Their pain must be acknowledged and addressed with compassion.

Stories of Redemption and Healing

Redemption is at the heart of God's story. Scripture shows examples of God restoring what was broken and bringing beauty from ashes. Consider Peter, who denied Jesus three times in His darkest hour. Peter's failure was profound, yet Jesus sought him out after the resurrection, restoring him with the words, *"**Feed my sheep**"* (*John 21:17*). Peter's redemption wasn't just about his relationship with Jesus—it was about empowering him to care for others and lead the early church.

In my life, I've experienced the profound healing that comes from confronting pain and seeking reconciliation. One relationship strained due to my calling was restored only after years of prayer and intentional effort. While the process was slow and, at times, painful, it ultimately led to a deeper understanding of God's grace and a stronger bond than before.

For those called, these stories of redemption aren't just examples to admire—they're invitations to hope. They remind us that no relationship is beyond God's reach, and no wound is too deep for His healing touch. The redemption process doesn't erase the past but transforms it. It uses what was meant for harm for God's glory. Just as Peter went on to boldly lead the church, we, too, can move forward from the pain of casualties with renewed purpose.

When Reconciliation Is Not Possible

In some cases, those affected by our journey may not be reachable or willing to engage in healing. Perhaps they've distanced themselves, or the opportunity for reconciliation has passed. In these moments, we must entrust the situation to God. We're reminded in **Romans 12:18: "If it is possible, as far as it depends on you, live at peace with everyone" (NIV)**.

When reconciliation isn't possible, we can pray for those we've hurt, asking God to bring healing to their hearts and peace to their lives. We can also learn from these experiences, ensuring we grow from them and avoid repeating the same mistakes. While we may not be able to repair every relationship or undo every harm, we can entrust these situations to the One who can bring peace and redemption in His time.

Job and David Revisited

As we turn our focus to healing, let us revisit the lives of Job and David—not to recount their losses, but to glean from their responses. What do their stories teach us about navigating the aftermath of casualties and finding restoration in the presence of God?

The Story of Job - Worship In The Face of Loss

In a previous chapter, we explored Job's remarkable endurance amidst unimaginable suffering. He lost his children, his wealth, and his health—all casualties of Satan's calculated attacks. Yet, Job's first response to this devastation was not to curse God, as Satan had predicted, but to fall on his face in worship, declaring, *"**The Lord gave, and the Lord has taken away; blessed be the name of the Lord" (Job 1:21, ESV)**.*

Job's posture of worship in the face of overwhelming loss served as an anchor for his soul. When his wife, sharing in their grief, urged him to curse God and die, Job refused to sin with his lips (*Job 2:10*). He chose instead to trust in God's sovereignty when he couldn't understand His ways.

For those who have experienced casualties in their calling, Job's story reminds us that worship is not about denying the reality of pain but about declaring the truth of God's goodness and faithfulness in the midst of it. Worship shifts our focus from the wounds to the One who can heal them. It positions our hearts to receive the strength, peace, and restoration only God can provide.

The Story of David - Worship Amidst Personal Responsibility

David's story also highlights a different dimension of casualties arising from our choices. His sin with Bathsheba and the subsequent fallout brought untold pain, not only to himself but also to his family and nation. From the death of his infant son to Absalom's rebellion, David carried the weight of knowing that his actions set these tragedies in motion. Yet, in his grief, David turned to worship. After the death of his child, David rose, washed, and went into the house of the Lord to worship (**2 Samuel 12:20**). His act of worship was not a denial of his pain but a declaration of his trust in God's righteousness. He acknowledged that while the consequences of his sin were real, God's mercy and faithfulness remained.

For those of us navigating the wounds caused by our failures, David's story offers hope. While the casualties of our actions cannot always be undone, worship provides a pathway to restoration. It allows us to realign our hearts with God, to seek His forgiveness, and to trust in His ability to bring beauty from ashes (**Isaiah 61:3**).

Learning From Their Pain

Job and David demonstrate the vital role of worship in the healing process. Worship isn't simply a response to God's blessings; it's an act of surrender that acknowledges His sovereignty in the face of loss. Whether the casualties are the result of spiritual warfare, like Job's, or our choices, like David's, worship anchors us in the truth of who God is and what He's able to do.

As you reflect on their lives, consider this:

- Job worshiped through his grief and confusion, and God restored him, blessing him with twice as much as he had (**Job 42:10**).

- David worshiped through guilt and loss, and God used his lineage to bring forth the Messiah, Jesus Christ.

Both men endured the wounds of their journeys, but their worship positioned them to experience God's healing and redemption.

Moving Forward

Revisiting these stories wasn't about observing their pain—it was about learning how to bring resolution to your own. Have you experienced casualties in your calling? Are you struggling to find hope amidst the wounds? Consider how worship can be a key to your healing.

- Worship invites God's presence into your brokenness, creating space for Him to bring comfort and restoration (**Psalm 34:18**).

- Worship shifts your perspective, reminding you that the God who allowed the trial also holds your future.

- Worship declares your trust in God when you don't have all the answers, enabling you to move forward in faith.

As you press on, remember the lessons from Job and David. Worship was their anchor—a way to process their pain and align their hearts with God's sovereignty. Their pain, though immense, wasn't the end of their story. Likewise, the casualties you face aren't the end of yours.

For those affected by the casualties, worship can also be a pathway to healing. While it may be difficult to worship in the midst of pain, it's in these moments that God draws near. **Psalm 34:18** reminds us, **"The Lord is close to the brokenhearted and saves those who are crushed in spirit"** (**NIV**). Worship opens the door for God's presence to bring comfort and renewal, even when the answers remain unclear.

For those called by God, worship is a vital step in healing. It acknowledges the pain without denying God's faithfulness. It shifts the focus from the casualties to the One who can bring restoration. In the posture of worship, you'll find strength, healing, and the assurance that God is working all things together for your good and His glory (**Romans 8:28**).

Steps To Healing

Healing is a journey, and every step requires intentionality. Here are steps to consider as you seek healing for yourself and those affected by your call:

1. Pray for Wisdom and Strength

Healing begins in the presence of God. **James 1:5** encourages us:

"If any of you lacks wisdom, let him ask God, who gives generously to all without reproach, and it will be given him" (**ESV**). Ask God for clarity about the wounds that need attention and the courage to address them. Prayer is not just a preparation for action—it's the action that paves the way for reconciliation and healing.

2. Take Responsibility

Own your part in the hurt, even if it was unintentional. Apologize sincerely without deflecting blame. **Proverbs 28:13** reminds us: *"Whoever conceals his transgressions will not prosper, but he who confesses and forsakes them will obtain mercy"* (**ESV**).

3. Extend Forgiveness

Just as we seek forgiveness from others, we must also be willing to forgive. Holding onto bitterness only deepens the wounds. **Colossians 3:13** instructs: *"Bear with each other and forgive one another if any of you has a grievance against someone. Forgive as the Lord forgave you"* (**NIV**).

4. Allow Time and Space

Healing doesn't happen overnight. Give others the time and space to process their pain while remaining open and available for reconciliation. Trust God to work in their hearts in His timing. **Ecclesiastes 3:1** reminds us: *"To everything there is a season, and a time to every purpose under the heaven"* (**KJV**).

5. Worship As A Healing Balm

In moments of pain, choose to worship. Worship shifts our focus from the wounds to the One who can heal them. As Job and David demonstrated, worship anchors us in God's goodness and reminds us that He's with us, even in the storm. **Psalm 34:1-3** encourages us to say: *"I will bless the Lord at all times; His praise shall continually be in my mouth. My soul shall make its boast in the Lord; The humble shall hear of it and be glad. Oh, magnify the Lord with me, and let us exalt His name together"* (**NKJV**).

6. Focus on Growth

Use the experience as a catalyst for growth. Reflect on what God is teaching you through the situation and how you can become a better steward of your calling. **Philippians 3:13-14** reminds us to keep pressing forward: *"Brothers and sisters, I do not consider myself yet to have taken hold of it. But one thing I do: Forgetting what is behind and straining toward what is ahead, I press on toward the goal to win the prize for which God has called me heavenward in Christ Jesus"* (**NIV**).

7. Entrust The Rest To God

When reconciliation isn't possible, entrust the situation to God. He's the ultimate healer, and His grace is sufficient to cover what we cannot fix. **Romans 12:18-19** says: *"If it is possible, as much as depends on you, live peaceably with all men. Beloved, do not avenge yourselves, but rather give place to wrath; for it is written, 'Vengeance is Mine, I will repay,' says the Lord"* (**NKJV**).

Impacted by the Call

For those who feel like they've been casualties in someone else's journey, know that your pain matters to God. He sees you, knows your heart, and longs to heal you. **Psalm 34:18** assures us: *"The Lord is close to the brokenhearted and saves those who are crushed in spirit"* (**NIV**). Allow God to minister to your heart, to bring you comfort and restoration. Seek Him in prayer, lean into His Word, and trust He's working all things together for your good.

For those who are called, the casualties of the journey can feel overwhelming, but they don't have to define us or the people affected by them. Healing from the wounds caused by our calling is not just about resolving the past—it's about stepping into the future with renewed strength and purpose. God's grace is sufficient for restoring and healing those we've hurt. Whether seeking healing for yourself or offering it to others, know that God's grace is sufficient for every step of the journey. This chapter is an invitation to take those first steps toward healing, trusting that God's redemption is greater than any wound.

As you reflect on this chapter, ask yourself:

- Who has been impacted by my journey, and how can I take steps toward reconciliation?

- What steps can I take to bring healing to those wounds?

- How can I invite God into this process, trusting Him to do what only He can do?

- What lesson is God teaching me through this experience that I can carry forward into my calling?

Healing from the wounds isn't a detour from the call—it's part of it. Just as Jesus bore the scars of His crucifixion as a testament to His love and sacrifice, our scars can become markers of God's grace and redemption. Let this be the season where healing begins, not only for you but for everyone touched by your journey. Let this chapter be the beginning of healing, a step toward redemption, and a testimony to the power of God's grace. No matter the wounds or casualties, God is faithful to restore, redeem, and use every part of your journey for His glory.

Whether the casualties in your life stem from spiritual battles, as with Job, or personal choices, as with David, healing is possible. By revisiting their stories through the lens of worship, you can find the courage to face your wounds and hope to move forward. Worship is not only a response to victory—it's the path to it. Let it guide you as you navigate the aftermath of casualties, trusting that the God who sustained Job and restored David will also sustain and restore you.

No man that warreth entangleth himself with the affairs of this life; that he may please him who hath chosen him to be a soldier.

(2 Timothy 2:4 KJV)

CASUALTIES OF THE CALL

CHAPTER 11

LIVING THE CALL

Chapter 11: "Living The Call"

The path of answering God's call is neither straightforward nor predictable. It demands perseverance, faith, and humility. As we draw near to the last chapter of this book, the focus now shifts to the daily practice of living the call— a life that embraces intentionality, resilience, and unwavering trust in the One who called us.

Answering God's call is not a momentary decision but a lifelong commitment. It means embracing the challenges, accepting the sacrifices, and allowing God to mold us through every season of the journey. More importantly, it means living in a way that reflects His glory and grace, serving as a light to a world desperately needing His truth and love.

A Lifelong Journey

The call is dynamic, evolving as we grow in our faith and understanding of God. At times, it can feel exhilarating, filled with purpose and clarity. At other times, it can feel like a weight, demanding more than we think we can give. But in every season, the call remains sacred, and our response to it shapes not only our lives but also the lives of those around us.

Hebrews 12:1-2 reminds us: *"Let us run with endurance the race that is set before us, looking unto Jesus, the author and finisher of our faith."* This verse captures the essence of living the call. It's a race that requires endurance, focus, and constant reliance on Jesus, who initiates and completes our journey.

The Purpose of Repetition

Throughout this book, we've revisited themes like obedience, casualties, spiritual warfare, and healing. This repetition is intentional—not to revisit the same lessons but to demonstrate how interconnected these truths are. Each theme builds upon the others, creating a holistic framework for living the call. The repetition is to take you to a panoramic view of the call.

Think of these themes as the threads of a tapestry. They may seem repetitive or disconnected, but when woven together, they form a masterpiece. God's call requires us to revisit these truths continually, allowing them to strengthen and refine us as we grow.

For example:

- **Obedience** anchors us in God's will, ensuring that we walk in alignment with His purpose.

- **Casualties** remind us of the cost of the call and the need for humility and vigilance.

- **Spiritual warfare** equips us to stand firm against the enemy's schemes.

- **Healing** restores us and others, enabling us to move forward with renewed strength.

Each of these themes isn't a step to be completed but a reality to be lived.

The Call In Every Season

Living the call means recognizing that each season brings unique opportunities and challenges. Here are a few perspectives to carry forward:

1. In Seasons of Waiting

Trust God's timing. As we've seen in Moses's life, delayed obedience or stepping out prematurely can lead to unnecessary pain. Waiting is not wasted when God prepares our hearts and circumstances for His perfect will.

2. In Seasons of Battle

Remember that spiritual warfare is a reality. Arm yourself daily with the armor of God (*Ephesians 6:10-18*), and remain vigilant against the enemy's schemes. As Paul reminds us in *2 Timothy 2:3-4*, endure hardship as a good soldier of Christ Jesus, focusing on the mission God has entrusted you with.

3. In Seasons of Healing

Embrace the healing process for yourself and those impacted by your journey. As explored in

Chapter 10, healing requires humility, intentionality, and the willingness to trust God's redemptive power.

4. In Seasons of Harvest

Celebrate the fruit of your obedience, giving all glory to God. Whether it's lives transformed, relationships restored, or hearts drawn closer to Him, remember that the harvest is His.

The Call of Intentionality

Living the call requires continually growing, adapting, and surrendering. It's a process that often begins with enthusiasm but evolves through seasons of trials, victories, and moments of doubt. This is why Jesus invites us to follow Him daily, taking up our cross and denying ourselves (**Luke 9:23**).

This process is deeply personal and profoundly relational. Our lives, as called individuals, intersect with the lives of others, creating opportunities for healing and impact. The call of God isn't only about fulfilling a mission; it's about becoming the person He created you to be.

Living the call isn't about perfection; it's about faithfulness. It's about waking up each day and surrendering to God's will, trusting Him to guide you through every challenge and every victory.

Here are a few ways to live the call with intentionality:

1. Stay Anchored In Worship

Worship is not just a response to God's blessings; it's a declaration of His sovereignty, even in the midst of trials. As we've seen in the lives of Job and David, worship has the power to anchor us in God's presence, shift our focus from our circumstances to His goodness, and invite His healing into our lives.

2. Embrace Obedience Daily

Obedience is not a one-time act; it's a daily choice. Whether we follow a specific prompting from God or live in alignment with His Word, obedience keeps us in step with His purpose.

3. Accept The Cost

The call of God comes with a cost, but it's worth bearing. As Jesus said in **Matthew 16:25**, *"For whoever wants to save their life will lose it, but whoever loses their life for me will find it"* (**NIV**). Accepting the cost is an act of trust, believing that God's plans are greater than our sacrifices.

4. Cultivate Resilience

Resilience is essential for enduring the challenges of the call. As Paul reminds us in **2 Timothy 2:3-4**, *"Endure hardship as a good soldier of Christ Jesus. No one serving as a soldier gets entangled in civilian affairs, but rather tries to please his commanding officer"* (**NIV**). Resilience allows us to stay focused, avoiding the distractions that weaken our resolve. I will speak more about this in the next chapter.

A Call To Action

Living the call isn't just about looking back—it's about moving forward with courage and faith. As you reflect on the lessons of this book, consider the following questions:

- How can I apply these lessons to my daily life?

- Who needs to experience the healing and redemption of God's grace through me?

- Am I fully surrendered to God's will, ready to embrace both the cost and the blessings of the call?

The call of God is not a burden; it's a privilege. It's an invitation to partner with Him in His work, to bring light into darkness, and to reflect His glory in a broken world.

Living As A Victorious Warrior

Victory in the call is not about avoiding battles or casualties—it's about standing firm in the midst of them and trusting God to work through every challenge, failure, and moment of surrender. As we've seen throughout this book, God faithfully redeems every part of our journey, using the wounds and scars to display His grace and power.

Romans 8:28 assures us: *"And we know that in all things God works for the good of those who love him, who have been called according to his purpose"* (NIV).

As you move forward, let this truth guide you. The call is not about perfection; it's about faithfulness. It's not about never falling; it's about getting back up. And it's not about avoiding pain but finding purpose in the midst of it.

CASUALTIES OF THE CALL
CHAPTER 12
THE REWARD OF ENDURANCE

Chapter 12: The Reward of Endurance

As we come to the final chapter of this book, it's time to step back and see the journey as a whole. Throughout this book, we have examined the realities of the call—the sacrifices, the struggles, and the casualties that come with it all. But as we bring this journey to a close, it is crucial to remember that **God does not leave His faithful ones without reward.** The trials, losses, and battles are not the final chapter of our story. **For every sacrifice, there is a promise. For every tear shed, there is restoration. For every battle fought, there is a victory waiting on the other side.**

God has never called anyone into purpose without **the promise of a reward.** This is the foundation of endurance—the certainty that, **despite the pain, something greater is coming.** The key is perseverance—not giving up in the face of adversity, not allowing hardship to define our destiny, and not letting weariness rob us of what God has promised.

Endurance: The Mark of the Called

When God calls, He is not merely looking for someone who will start the journey—**He is looking for those who will finish.** The weight of the call requires endurance because **every promise comes with a process.** Many people begin with excitement and zeal, but when opposition arises, some fall away. The ones who press through the fire, however, **are the ones who will taste the fruit of their faithfulness.**

Paul writes in **Galatians 6:9**, *"And let us not grow weary in well doing: for in due season we shall reap, if we faint not."* The condition of the promise is **not growing weary**—not allowing the pressures, losses, and disappointments to make us abandon our purpose.

Endurance is what separates those who merely hear the call from those who **fulfill it.**

- **Moses** endured forty years in the wilderness before stepping into his purpose.

- **Joseph** suffered betrayal, slavery, and imprisonment before reaching the palace.

- **David** faced years of running from Saul before being crowned king.

- **Paul** was beaten, imprisoned, and persecuted before finishing his race.

- **Jesus Himself** endured the cross because of **the joy set before Him (Hebrews 12:2).**

Each of them had a choice—to surrender to the process or to abandon the call. **They endured, and they received the reward.**

The Unseen Work of Endurance

One of the hardest truths about endurance is that **much of the process happens in silence.**

As mentioned before in Chapter 2, when a seed is planted, it is buried deep beneath the soil. To the natural eye, it looks like **nothing is happening.** But beneath the surface, a transformation is taking place. The seed's outer shell must die and break apart before new life can emerge.

In the same way, **our endurance often feels hidden.** It feels like no one sees the battles we fight, the sacrifices we make, or the prayers we cry out in private. But **God sees.**

1 Corinthians 15:58 declares, ***"Therefore, my beloved brethren, be steadfast, unmovable, always abounding in the work of the Lord, for as much as ye know that your labor is not in vain in the Lord."***

What looks like a season of **burial is actually a season of preparation.** Your endurance is not wasted. The trials that feel like they are breaking you are actually making way for **your next level of growth.**

The Reward of Endurance in Scripture

Throughout Scripture, we see that God never allows His faithful ones to **endure in vain.** The pattern is clear: **great suffering is often followed by great reward.**

- **Joseph** endured betrayal, slavery, and imprisonment, but one day **God shifted everything.** In an instant, he was promoted from the prison to the palace **(Genesis 41:41)**. His faithfulness positioned him to save an entire nation.

- **David** was anointed as king but spent years running for his life before taking the throne. Yet when his season of endurance was complete, **God established his kingdom forever.**

- **Job** lost everything—his children, his wealth, his health. But because he **did not lose his faith**, God restored double what he had before **(Job 42:10)**.

- **Paul** suffered beatings, shipwrecks, and imprisonments, yet he boldly declared, *"I have fought the good fight, I have finished the race, I have kept the faith. Henceforth there is laid up for me the crown of righteousness"* (2 Timothy 4:7-8, ESV).

Even **Jesus** endured suffering because He knew **the reward on the other side. "For the joy that was set before Him, He endured the cross" (Hebrews 12:2).** His suffering led to **our salvation.**

God is a Restorer

The enemy wants us to believe that what we've lost **can never be restored.** That the pain we've endured **is permanent.** That the relationships that have suffered **can never be healed.** But **this is a lie.**

God is not only a redeemer—**He is a restorer.**

Job's story is one of the most powerful reminders of this truth. After losing everything, Job continued to trust God, and in the end, **God restored double what he had lost.**

Joel 2:25 declares, *"And I will restore to you the years that the locust hath eaten."*

If you have experienced casualties because of your calling, **do not believe the lie that it is over.** Your endurance is setting the stage for **divine restoration.**

The Eternal Perspective: A Greater Reward Awaits

One of the greatest deceptions of the enemy is to make us focus so much on the pain of today that we forget about the reward of tomorrow. **But the greatest rewards are not found in this life—they are eternal.**

Jesus said in **Matthew 5:12**, *"Rejoice and be glad, for your reward is great in heaven."*

Paul echoes this in **Romans 8:18**, *"For I consider that the sufferings of this present time are not worth comparing with the glory that is to be revealed to us."*

This world is temporary. The hardships we endure here **cannot compare to the reward that is coming.**

Strength in Weakness

Endurance is not merely about surviving hardship; it is about emerging from the struggle transformed. Some battles don't end with immediate victory—some leave us with lasting reminders of what we have endured. There are times when God brings healing and complete restoration, and there are times when He allows us to carry the marks of our struggles, using them as testimonies of His sustaining grace. Two powerful biblical examples of this are **Jacob and Paul.**

Jacob's defining moment came when he **wrestled with God** at Peniel **(Genesis 32:24-30)**. He had spent his life grasping—first at his brother's heel, then at blessings, and later at wealth. But in this moment, he found himself wrestling not with man, but with God Himself. The struggle lasted all night, and Jacob refused to let go until he received a blessing. However, **that blessing came with a cost**—God touched Jacob's hip, permanently dislocating it. From that moment forward, Jacob walked with a limp, leaning on a staff for the rest of his life.

God could have healed Jacob's hip instantly, but He didn't. Instead, He allowed Jacob to bear the **mark of that encounter** as a constant reminder of **who he was before and who he had become through God's transforming power**. His limp was not a sign of weakness; it was a sign of his **dependence on God.** No longer would he walk in his own strength—he would now lean on God for every step he took.

Paul also understood what it meant to **live with an affliction that God chose not to remove.** He spoke of a **"thorn in the flesh, a messenger of Satan sent to buffet him"** (2 Corinthians 12:7). Though he pleaded with God three times to remove it, God's response was not what Paul expected:

"My grace is sufficient for you, for My strength is made perfect in weakness." (2 Corinthians 12:9, NKJV)

Rather than removing the affliction, God gave Paul the strength to endure it. **God was teaching him that divine power is best demonstrated when human strength fails.** Like Jacob, Paul had to rely completely on God to sustain him.

For many of us, this is a difficult truth to accept. We want God to take away the pain, to heal the wound, to remove the struggle. But sometimes, **He chooses to leave it—not to harm us, but to remind us that His grace is enough.** Some struggles are meant to shape us, to humble us, and to draw us closer to Him.

Jacob walked with a staff. Paul carried a thorn. Both were **evidence of their endurance**—marks of men who encountered God and were forever changed. Their examples remind us that not every battle ends with the removal of the hardship. **Sometimes, the reward of endurance is the strength to keep walking with the limp, knowing that God's power is carrying us forward.**

A Call to Finish the Race

Every person called by God must decide: **Will I endure?**

Will I trust God when it's hard? Will I remain faithful even when it seems like nothing is changing? Will I continue pressing forward when everything in me wants to give up?

Paul's charge in **1 Corinthians 9:24** is clear:

"Do you not know that in a race all the runners run, but only one receives the prize? So run that you may obtain it."

This is the challenge for every believer. **The cost of the call is real, but so is the reward.**

Final Reflection

As you close this book, take a moment to ask yourself:

- Have I truly embraced the endurance required for my calling?

- Am I trusting God for restoration, even after loss?

- Do I see my suffering through an eternal perspective?

- Will I finish my race, no matter what?

The reward of endurance is not just about what you will receive in this life—**it is about the legacy you leave and the eternity you will inherit.**

Stay the course. Keep fighting. Keep believing.

The One who called you is faithful, and **He will bring you to your expected end (Jeremiah 29:11).**

You are not running in vain. Endure. Finish strong. The reward is waiting.

The Benediction

May the God who called you, sustain you in every trial, strengthen you in every battle, and heal you from every wound. May His grace empower you to endure the call with courage, humility, and faithfulness, bringing glory to His name and hope to those around you. May you always remember that the One who began a good work in you will carry it to completion until the day of Christ Jesus (*Philippians 1:6*).

Go forth, not in your strength, but in His, knowing that you're called, equipped, and loved by the One who holds all things in His hands. **In Jesus name, Amen.**

CASUALTIES
OF
THE CALL

Made in the USA
Monee, IL
02 March 2025